How To Think And Become A Successful Webpreneur

Richard Essi

ISBN:1477613749
ISBN-13: **978-1477613740**

DEDICATION

I would like to dedicate this book to my ever so loving and patient wife Diane, and my two children Daniel, and Niyah. Thank you for your support and continue to dream bigger with every passing day.

CONTENTS

	Acknowledgments	i
1	In The Gutter	1
2	Beware Of Wolves In Sheep's Clothing	Pg 11
3	Relax, You Are On The Right Track	Pg 24
4	Your Body Is Your Slave, Not Your Master	Pg 32
5	Who Are You, And What Is Your Purpose?	Pg 48
6	Becoming A Successful Entrepreneur Is A Choice	Pg 54
7	Why Conviction Always Beats Obligation	Pg 61
8	Discover The Real Power Of Enthusiasm	Pg 71
9	Integrity Vs. Manipulation	Pg 75
10	The Power Of Authentic Relational Marketing	Pg 99

Contents

ACKNOWLEDGMENTS

This book would not have been possible without the inspiration of my mentors...you know yourselves! Thank you Mom and Dad for giving me the opportunity to discover a world bigger than my culture. I am eternally grateful to the Almighty God for the intervention of His Sovereign hand in my life, without which I won't be where I am today.

1 **IN THE GUTTER**

I still remember this moment of my life like it was yesterday.

I had been unemployed for about two straight years with no unemployment benefits, except from a few monetary gifts I occasionally received from my parents and a few church family members.

It was one of the lowest points of my life. I had willfully walked away from a 70,000 USD/year job immediately after my wedding. My wife and I were living in a tiny studio, and bumped into each other every time we stood up and moved within the apartment.

Needless, to say that the challenges of marriage as a young couple, in addition to the other issues such as…. always being in the red, and never having enough to pay the bills, or yet again having to answer to the in laws about my jobless situation, were just some of the issues I found myself dealing with between November of 2003 and December of 2005.

Those were two long years that stretched, and molded me beyond recognition. Part of whom I am today is directly linked to the intense hardship I endured during this period.

I had walked away from a "dream" job with my wife's permission, because she had seen me break down in tears due to the mobbing and abuse that was taking place at my job.

If a strong and confident guy like me could be broken down like that, then it must have been serious. She was extremely supportive and encouraging.

Nevertheless, I will never forget the feeling I had one day when I came back home during this period.

I had found an "amazing opportunity" online that was supposedly a real High Yield Investment Program. HSBC bank, Loyal Bank in the Bahamas and a few other big names appeared to be part of this investment program.

I had personally spoken and met some members who had made multiple 6-figures from this opportunity.

Needless to say that I had dived in head first, and had even talked to my folks, and many of my close friends about this. The name of this program was called PIPS (People In Profits System). They were headquartered in Malaysia and even had Maestro Debit cards for ATM withdrawals anywhere in the world.

Being as desperate as we were, I had maxed out my credit card which had a limit of 5000 USD to really make it big with this opportunity and finally get out of all the debt and lack that we had been dragging along since my wife and I were still fiancées.

In fact, some of the friends I had recommended this opportunity to had actually succeeded in withdrawing more than 17,000+ USD with about 1000 USD invested. So you can imagine how exited I was feeling knowing that I had invested more.

I was actually so confident about this opportunity that I had gone ahead and bought a new BMW 528i from a friend of mine for 18,000 USD, reassuring him that I was going to pay for the car in a few months time.

How To Think And Become A Successful Webpreneur

Little did I know that I had just incurred an additional 18K USD of debt, that I was going to deeply regret.

A few weeks after this purchase, I received an e-mail notification about the arrest of Bryan Marsden the CEO of PIPS in Malaysia.

The news was shocking! I still remember how my heart sank, and how dizzy I felt just reading that e-mail....this could not possibly be happening!

This was just bad dream, and I would soon wake up!

No! It was not a bad dream, it was real. It was just the simple truth.

The whole scam had crumbled down!

I was in complete denial for the next few months, as I was convinced this was just a little mix up that would soon be ironed out.

It's not until I saw the pictures of Bryan and his wife Sharon in the local prison attire that it began to sink in.

I had lost money! Not only my money, but a lot of other people's money. Plus, I was the main go-to guy for information on PIPS.

What was I going to tell them?

Here I was sitting in my newly acquired BMW 528i feeling like a complete idiot and loser!

How could I have been so gullible, and so stupid at the same time! I just could not forgive myself!

Was this a lesson that I was receiving for being too greedy, desperate and gullible?

Was I ever going to make any money on this Internet that I had discovered in 1997?

Richard Essi

How could I have been on the Internet for these many years, and still not have anything to show for it.

Maybe I was meant to just be a regular employee with a 9-5 job. Maybe I was not grateful enough. Maybe I just needed to stop dreaming and dragging my family into the gutters of gloom and despair.

What about my wife who had been extremely patient and understanding up till now....how was she going to take this?

Would my marriage withstand this?

It is on one of these days, a few days after the "breaking news" about Bryan's arrest that I came home to find my wife in tears.

She was sitting on the table.

The table was littered with bills, and more bills! She was overwhelmed, and did not know what to do.

She had hoped that my various "Internet projects" were going to help pay the bills!

Now she was completely shattered!

When I walked in through the door, our eyes crossed, and she burst out into even more tears.

I still remember very clearly what she said to me.

She had said:

"Honey....what are we going to do?" with a quivering voice.

I knew right then and there that I had to go back to a 9-5 job, and probably within the same backstabbing environment that had caused me to flee in the first place.

All this, was just too much for me! Seeing my wife in that state killed me!

How To Think And Become A Successful Webpreneur

So, I immediately went out and found another 9-5 job in the exact same toxic environment that I absolutely dreaded.

However, this time around, my wife's tears were my driving motivation.

For about a year or so, I did not touch the Internet, apart from check my mail, and watch movies or music clips.

I did not want to see **anything** about making money online.

To me, everybody making money online was a scam artist, and to make money online was to be a scam artist, and I didn't want to be one.

It is only a year or so later that I started looking online again at different ways to make a living from the Internet.

I wanted to steer clear of the get rich quick schemes and all those pie- in the sky gimmicks.

I now decided that I would treat all this information on making money like a Masters Program.

Over the years, I think I have invested over 50,000+ USD in products, courses, software, coaching, and seminars.

My conclusion after having bought from the gurus and the non-gurus, is that, there is no big secret golden key that you must find to open the treasure chest.

No, the common traits, principles, actions and philosophies I found in these guys was that they ALL had **the right success mind set**.

The right success mindset consists of having a philosophy and an ethical code, where values, principles, character, integrity, patience and genuine care is the real foundation for authentic and sustainable success.

This is what I now teach and write about, and I continue to look forward to meeting like-minded individuals who are doing the same thing or who want to do the same.

Richard Essi

Introducing Myself...

My Name is Richard Essi, and I originally hail from Cameroon, Central Africa.

In my short but rich 36 years on this earth I have had the privilege of living and visiting several countries around the world. A few of the countries include:

The United Kingdom, Scotland, Switzerland, The United States of America, Sierra Leone, Germany, Holland, France, Bulgaria, Sweden, Burundi, Guadeloupe, Denmark, Belgium, Equatorial Guinea, Italy, Canada and many more scheduled.

The richness of the cultures, the people and the experiences have had a profound impact on my mindset and my perception of life.

If I could use one word to describe the overall impact, I would say...EMPOWERED!

It is from this world view that I have developed a life philosophy that I have gladly shared with my audiences, friends and relatives, and it is a great pleasure to now share a few of these concepts as applies to starting and running an Internet business with you.

I currently live in the beautiful city of Geneva, Switzerland.

I am above all other titles, a husband to my beautiful wife, Diane, and a father to my two gorgeous kids, Daniel (5 years) and Niyah (19 months).

This is now, but it all started back then.

You see, back in the day, the very idea of creating and having a business running on the internet with nothing more than a computer and an internet connection was always intriguing and fascinating to me.

How To Think And Become A Successful Webpreneur

I mean think about it....all you need to have is your internet connection and a laptop or a desktop computer, and from your living room or from your home office you are able to run a business without all the physical overhead one is used to seeing in a traditional brick and mortar business.

Like I mentioned earlier, this concept had always seemed far-fetched but at the same time extremely intriguing for me – back then in 1997.

Ok, to put things in perspective you have to understand that I was a young foreign student from Cameroon, Central Africa discovering the unlimited world of opportunities that was now opening to me in this new country that would soon become my second home.

When I was still back in Cameroon, having an internet connection was like something right out of an alien or science fiction movie.

How could you possibly connect to some "virtual world" and start to relate with people from all around the world? It was a concept that was just difficult to grasp.

So there I was in the United States of America.....in Chicago to be specific studying to obtain a Bachelor of Science degree in Telecommunications Management, at the DeVry University and I was discovering the technological world and the unlimited possibilities that it presented.

That's when things really began to make sense for me. Many of the friends I made were guys and girls who were doing all kinds of stuff online (Forex, S&P 500 Mini contracts, internet marketing etc)

So, my friends and I started to hang out in forums, discussion boards meeting and connecting with new and like minded people. That's when we realized that we could actually have some sort of a parallel life on the Internet.

It was truly exciting.. this was taking the "pen pal" concept to a whole new level !

This was of course back in the day when spending too much time on the Internet was considered "geeky" and "anti-social".

So, the moment I started to passionately talk about the Internet, and all the different things you could do on the Internet, I always had the same systematic response....

...eyebrows raised, and a

"poor thing....he doesn't have any friends..." look.

That was in the late 90's and early 2000's

Well, today, the tide has changed.

If you don't have a Face book, Twitter or LinkedIn account, or any of these social network accounts, you are probably going to get a similar look and in some cases, the exact same phrase !

You see, after the dotcom boom in the early nineties, most people thought that this whole technology craze was a scam, and was too virtual to be real and profitable.

Everybody was watching all these start-up companies sucking in millions and millions of dollars only to have all that money evaporate into thin air!

Even though Yahoo was one of the highly successful startups from the dotcom era, it wasn't until the arrival of powerhouses like **Google**, **Ebay** and **Amazon** that everybody started to take the Internet a little bit more seriously.

People were reliant on the yellow pages for the most accurate information. Everything was still very paper based.

There were a few search engines apart from Yahoo such as metacrawler.com, ask.com and lycos.com and many more who were trying to give the Internet some credibility and legitimacy.

However, the arrival of the above mentioned giants (**Google, Ebay** and **Amazon**) simply closed the debate on whether or not the Internet could be taken seriously.

It is estimated that today 300 + million people use Google every day to search for information.

I am sure you remember the days when "e-commerce" was the buzz word. Everybody was talking about this without really understanding what it meant, but it was just "cool" to be associated with the term.

Those who grasped this e-commerce concept understood that it was all about having an online store and selling to a market that was no longer limited to your geographical region, but one that was open to the entire world.

This created a completely new profession – A certified Ebay Seller.

This phenomena exploded on the scene and people started discovering and using the power of Ebay to earn extra income, and there are literally millions of people today who now earn a full time income from simply buying and selling on the Internet.

However, selling on Ebay is far from the only way to make money on the Internet.

I remember being asked about 10 years ago by a close friend of mine what exactly I was doing to earn some extra income on the Internet (In my excitement I had of course told her about my Internet Marketing passion).

Before I could even answer her, I remember her blurting out…. *"Oh…you are doing the Ebay thingy?"*

Well, what was I going to say?

It was not just E-bay, I was doing several other things, but the more I tried to explain to my friends and relatives, the more confused they would be, so I usually just went with their flow and took whatever name they wanted to call it.

If you can remotely relate to my story, then you have the makings of a pioneer in your circle of influence.

"To be great is to be misunderstood" - Ralph Waldo Emerson

"Any man who knows all the answers most likely misunderstood the questions"

"Any man who afflicts the human race with ideas must be prepared to see them misunderstood" - Henry Louis Mencken

2 BEWARE OF THE WOLVES IN SHEEP'S CLOTHING

Fast forward to 2011, and I am still in front of my computer with an Internet connection, albeit 20x faster!

However, today, I work from home. My clients and partners are scattered all over the globe and in different time zones, and they are just a Skype away.

In other words, I have been around long enough to have seen most of the good and the bad on the Internet.

Not only have I seen the good and the bad, but I have also experienced the good and the bad, and it is out of all the richness of the process of my journey that I have decided to give back as generously as possible.

While the Internet continues to establish itself as the new land of opportunity, we all know that where there are opportunities, there are also numerous traps.

One of the primary objectives in providing you with this book is to give you a **mindset of STEEL**.

One that will help you steer clear of the pitfalls that many have fallen into and have never been able to recover.

You need to know that there are people (wolves) out there who make a living by preying on desperate people.

These "wolves" follow the blood trail...

Desperate people leave trail tracks. They ask certain kind of questions on forums. They type in certain key phrases in the search engines. They leave certain kind of comments on blogs.

Unfortunately, there are web entrepreneurs who are more concerned about milking the cow dry rather than making sure that the cow continues to be well fed in order to continue producing more milk.

Not being aware of this will make you an easy prey for these wolves in sheep's clothing, that have words that are sweeter than honey, and that know how to press all the right buttons to get you emotionally juiced and ready to bleed your credit card to death !

If you don't already know, then you should be aware that it can be a real jungle out there when you don't know who to trust and what information to implement.

The wealth of information available can and will be extremely overwhelming if you don't know how to separate the apples from the oranges, and in many cases the rotten apples from the rotten oranges.

In this book, you will discover the indispensable approach and mindset you will need to establish and grow your business online to ensure that you obtain **long term success**. This approach will of course crash against the status quo where the dominant philosophy is **"make big money quick and get out"** and **"the end justifies the means."**

In my 15 years online I have come to the conclusion that there are certain values and principles that stand the test of time and <u>always</u> will. <u>This is where the majority of newbie Internet Entrepreneurs miss the boat!</u>

As mentioned earlier, **Integrity, honesty, authenticity, genuine care and concern, having a true listening ear, respecting and treating people like**

How To Think And Become A Successful Webpreneur

you would want to be treated etc. are the true iron pillars that will make you succeed beyond your wildest imagination.

These values work and have constituted the invisible platform or foundation on which many discreet and ethical online millionaires have built AND maintained their business for decades.

This is also how I have done business over the years, and this is what you will learn to implement.

Using the Internet to make a quick buck online is one thing. Having, an ethical and sustainable internet business that you can be proud of passing on to the next generation is another story.

What you will discover, learn and implement in this book are methods that have been tried and have passed the test of time and profitability, no matter the product or service you are selling online.

There are lessons learnt from my failures (a lot of them actually!) and my successes, and many of them from my clients and associates. So, you are going to benefit from a wealth of information that will have only one objective – **to empower you**.

I am going to save you time, money and lots of unnecessary effort. This book will only by useful if you truly apply the principles and concepts.

What I can assure you is that by focusing on the mindset required for the newbie Web entrepreneur you will cut your learning curve significantly and come out way ahead of 95% of the people who continue to struggle to start and build an Internet business.

I do not like hype and I am convinced you don't either. So, don't expect to see any outrageous claims anywhere in this book or in any of my products for that matter.

One of the principles I live by is called the Iceberg principle.

Basically, what this means is that what you see is only 10 % of what really exists. The other 90% remains invisible to the human eye.

This iceberg principle is a philosophy that applies to all the areas of my life, and my business is no exception.

My intention is to over deliver in quality and resources, and sow seeds of hope, motivation for financial freedom and inspiration to never give up in order that you too may succeed in this new Internet economy.

If you think that you are arriving late to the game, and that there is no more money to be made, and that all the good Ideas have already been taken, then I can tell you right now that you are looking at things from the wrong angle.

You sound exactly like the investors who had a chance to invest in Microsoft or Google, but didn't and thought that it was all over. They never saw Face book or YouTube coming!

Believe me, you are not late. In fact, you are just on time!

One of the major mistakes I have seen made by the average "wanna be" entrepreneur on the Internet is not taking the time to evaluate and plan accordingly before diving into a business opportunity or starting an online business.

You will be surprised at the number of people who embark on an elaborate business with a substantial risk for loss without having factored all the eventualities, and without an appropriate response or backup plan to the various problems that could be encountered.

Think about it this way, would you send your 14 year old son or daughter alone in a camp you know nothing about in some forest you have never heard of, with friends you know absolutely nothing about without telling them anything apart from the fact that they are going to have lots of fun?

How To Think And Become A Successful Webpreneur

Would you send them out like that without having a "talk" about all the rules and the possible eventualities and what to do in case of an emergency?

I know for a fact that personally, I would think long and hard before sending my kids to a vacation camp for which I had no knowledge or information. And if I eventually did, it would be with a million precautions and back up plans if things did not go well.

What if today, your plan was to start a pizzeria in your neighborhood, would you just go out there and start paying rent and buying all the equipment that goes into starting a pizzeria?

I don't think so.

I think you would first want to evaluate your financial commitment, make a business plan and see if this is something that you can do.

You would sit down with your significant other and discuss this before making a decision right? So, why does it have to be different when it comes down to starting and running a business on the Internet?

Please consider the following points to help you determine how you are going to now start and run your Internet business. You will most likely not have any overhead, employees, or any other brick and mortar related expenses, but YOU WILL have expenses, and you need to consider them.

Here are the basic essentials:

A Unique Voice
It doesn't really matter what you sell on the Internet. Whether it be a physical item, a course on gardening, or a service.

It doesn't even matter if your market is already very competitive.

What truly matters is not necessarily what you say, it is how you say it. That is definitely what will make you stand out from the crowd.

Richard Essi

You have a way of saying and doing things that while it might resemble certain people, it is unlike anything else on this planet – it is unique.

That uniqueness can only manifest itself, when you get your mind right, and start thinking according to the true potential that is in you, and that is where your confidence, charisma and true personality will emerge.

Many live in the shadow of themselves. In the shadow of their past, their fears, and their future.

Stepping into a place of competence starts by knowing that you are capable and worthy of occupying such a position.

I remember back in the day when I had just graduated from University.

Like everybody else, I was trying to find a high-paying job.

What made me land some amazing interviews in a few fortune 500 companies was my unique presentation and image skills.

The class they had taught us on how to manage your image and how to present yourself was one that I had greatly enjoyed.

Whatever your skill, perfect it, and give it out as generously as you can in your own voice and watch what happens.

So, my CV, though professional, was original. In everything that I did, I always managed to find a way to stick out from the rest of the crowd that sent in the same lame Cvs and who sounded like robots in their interviews.

It felt good to be able to share some of the techniques I was using to help some of my friends land more interviews.

Well, on the Internet it is the same thing. You have to be unique. The value and skill you share with others has to have your unique fingerprint.

You don't need to re-invent the wheel, you just need to <u>embellish</u> it!

How To Think And Become A Successful Webpreneur

So, you need to of course look at what your competition is doing, and use that to your advantage, but a big part of your unique selling point should be your personal touch!

Once you are clear on this, you may now go ahead and reserve a domain name(Internet name) and get your site live on the web with the right hosting company.

Let me quickly and briefly go over this:

Domain Name and Hosting

A domain name is the equivalent of a title deed for a land on which you are going to build a house.

So, basically you are going to tell all the real estate agents of the Internet that you are going to be building a house soon, and that you are putting the necessary down payment to reserve this land for what you are going to be building.

There are many schools of thought on the type of domain name that should be chosen.

Some say that you need to choose a domain name that is linked to a keyword in the niche or in the field that you will be in. Others say it is more about the originality of the domain name.

For example, a site like cars.com will obviously be talking about cars, and it already contains the keyword « car » while a site like Google or yahoo doesn't really sound like a search engine.

What I have discovered is that if you have the most relevant domain name, but your site is lacking in relevancy, then your site will still not rank high even if you have the right keywords in your domain name.

You have to remember that Google's objective is to give its searchers the most accurate information, and not the most accurate domain name.

Google wants their users to keep coming back for more accurate and relevant information. That is why Google values sites that are rich with content in order to satisfy their search clients.

When you use the Internet to search for information, what you care the most about is the information that you will receive from the site that will solve your problem or answer your question right?

Using the same examples above, if you were to go to cars.com and find more motorcycles than cars, you will end up going to a site that offered you a selection of more cars even if the name of the site was NOT relevant to the content right?

The beauty of the domain name registration is that it doesn't cost as much as what it would cost to buy and reserve a land to build on here in the physical world.

The important detail to take note of with the domain name registration is that your domain has to be renewed. This could be every 1-5 years.

If you do not renew your domain name, on time, then your domain will go back out into the market and will be available for anybody to purchase.

So failure to renew your domain name will not only cause you to lose your domain for good, but you will find yourself in the worst of situations especially if you have taken the time to really build your business, and that you have plenty of targeted traffic coming to the site.

You will then find yourself having to chase the new owner to buy back your domain, and believe me you will pay a hefty sum, unless you can negotiate a deal with the owner.

Trust me, this has happened more times than you can imagine!

Now on to Hosting...
In very simple terms, hosting, is what puts your website online.

How To Think And Become A Successful Webpreneur

It is the activation of your domain name.

So for example let's say you have an idea for a project but you don't know when you are going to kick it off.

What you can start with is to reserve the domain name. Once you reserve the domain name, you have now blocked anybody else from picking up that domain.

There is nothing more annoying than having a fantastic business idea to develop online only to find out that the domain name that would have been an ideal match for your business has been taken.

Nevertheless, don't worry. There are still millions of domain names to be bought and reserved.

Today out of all the Internet user population (2.1 Billion), there are only 136+ million domain names worldwide. Which means that there is plenty of room for you.

Most of the three, four, five and six letter domain names have already been taken, but if you get a little creative you can really pick up a nice domain name for your business.

You can never go wrong with buying domain names.

As a matter of fact, there are people who make it their business to buy and sell domain names.

The buying and selling of domain names is more than a billion dollar industry.

What About A Blog?
This without a doubt is the most important piece of virtual real estate you will ever own.

It is your avenue to express your unique voice.

Don't worry about all the other blogs online.

I have seen people succeed with free blogs, and I have also seen people succeed with premium blogs.

I personally recommend having a premium blog right from the start. This way you will have full control over all your content at all times, and this will become vital when you start growing.

What you have to say is important. Your experience and points of view are unique

I personally highly recommend the Woo themes. They are not only elegant, but they are also very web compliant and they load fast.

An Auto Responder

An auto responder is simply a 24/7 secretary that helps you stay in touch with your readers/customers.

Auto responders are huge databases that store the e-mail addresses of the people that show interest in your writings or your products and services.

You can pre-program messages to be sent to your subscribers, or you can send out messages any time you want and all of them will receive a customized message from you.

My auto responder of choice is Getresponse.

If you are going to be spending money on anything to get started, it should be with the above mentioned tools.

You seriously do not need anything more.

You can then start learning all you need to learn about your field, your market and how to reach them with your value and expertise.

How To Think And Become A Successful Webpreneur

Your most important training will be what you are now receiving which is your mindset!

Don't go out buying all the products out there. You will simply create a big dent in your credit card.

I can recommend all kinds of blogs and forums where you can find a wealth of information for free.

It will simply take a lot of dedication and hard work, but with the right mindset you will succeed beyond your wildest dreams.

You have to understand that all the courses that are packaged and sold out there contain information that can mostly be found find for free on the Internet.

What gives these technical products (training, seminars, courses etc) their value is that they will mostly save you time.

In other words, someone has taken the time to assemble all this dispersed information into one comprehensible guide or manual, and this is what you pay for.

The information that is scattered all over the internet in forums and blog posts has been assembled, systematized and packaged for YOUR convenience. That's it!

I am telling you this so that you do not over estimate these products, and also so that you understand the pricing mechanism behind.

So, do not have any false expectations and do NOT fall for all the hype!

Don't believe it!

Believe me, you will find all kinds of hyped up income claims out there, and most with "proof".

Know that for each proof of success, there is 10 times more proof of failure.

Let me give you an example.

There are some neighborhoods in certain underdeveloped African countries that could compete with the best neighborhood in any western city....believe me!

The level of luxury is equal to or in some cases superior to what you will find in some the most developed countries.

The reality however is that these neighborhoods reflect the lifestyle of only 5% of the local population.

So it is with a lot of some of the hype you will see out there.

Over the years, I have seen many, many good people get burned and completely disillusioned with the whole concept of making a living from the Internet.

Now, I also believe that the blame is not only on the unscrupulous and sometimes shady web entrepreneurs out there, but it is also on us the customers.

You see, many of us like I was, enter this battlefield called making money on the Internet completely uninformed and unarmed.

If only I had taken that time to wear a helmet, a breastplate and a shield, I would have saved so much time, and avoided some unnecessary heart ache.

That's why you are truly in luck because you are getting the armor you need to face the adversities in the battle field of making money online, and you are more likely to win this war.

It will take A LOT of HARD WORK and effort, and you need to register that!

Like I mentioned earlier, the reason behind the positive mindset is so that you start believing that you have value to offer.

How To Think And Become A Successful Webpreneur

The hard work especially involves conditioning your mind to constantly seek to gain more value.

The more value you can give, the more wealth you will create.

In other words, the more you grow and develop, the more value you will have to offer, and the more you will be rewarded.

"All the so-called 'secrets of success' will not work unless you do" – Anonymous

"God gives every bird its food, but He does not throw it into its nest" - JG Holland

"The difference between try and triumph is a little umph" – Unknown

"I am a great believer in luck, and the harder I work the more I have of it." – Thomas Jefferson

"Opportunity is missed by most people because it is dressed in overalls and looks like work" – Thomas Edison

"The only place where success comes before work is in the dictionary" – Donald Kendall

"Hard work spotlights the character of people: some turn up their sleeves, some turn up their noses, some don't turn up at all" – Sam Ewing

3 **RELAX, YOU ARE ON THE RIGHT TRACK**

In this book I continually will be dealing a lot with the mindset and the motivation behind the actions that you will need to undertake as you build your Internet business.

Gone are the days where the web entrepreneur had to be a "computer geek" or some kind of "techie nerd".

You no longer have to be an IT genius or a gifted programmer to start and run your own successful Internet Business.

NO!....those days are over.

Today, some of the most successful web entrepreneurs are ordinary folks like you and me.

They all have one thing in common though...they have ideas and while many of them don't have ideas that are unique, they did find a UNIQUE way to express this common idea.

Today's entrepreneur is someone like you who is probably struggling to get out of the rut of monotony - out of the 9-5 rat race or the 24 /7 business owner.

How To Think And Become A Successful Webpreneur

There is a new era of opportunity on the Internet that is dawning on regular, and ordinary folks like you and me.

It doesn't matter if you use the Internet just to check your e-mail, and may be search for some info on Google.

It doesn't even matter if you don't have a Face book account.

There has been a major tipping point that has blown open the doors to tremendous financial freedom by starting and building a thriving business through the web.

This new breed of web Entrepreneurs now understand that achieving success, is all about having the appropriate mindset, like everything else in life.

These web entrepreneurs now understand that the same principles that apply to starting, building and managing a friendship, a marriage, and a family, are the same that are required to start and successfully run an Internet business.

The techniques, blueprints, and systems that are readily available are of no value if there is not the right mindset to implement them.

This is why you now need to be open and prepare to have a paradigm shift.

A Quick Reality Check For You
The State of the Economy

The state of the global economy today is no secret. Things are bad. In fact, things are really bad.

Many credible and renown analysts are predicting that things are going to get worse for quite a while, while there is another minority that says that things are going to get better soon.

Either way, all these are just studies and statistics, and no matter which study you choose to believe, you will still need to find an Internet business model that will work for you in good and bad times.

"The Internet will help achieve 'friction free capitalism' by putting buyer and seller in direct contact and providing more information to both about each other." - Bill Gates

As a matter of fact, if you really want to consider some statistics, consider the following:

|+| No. Of Internet Users worldwide – 2.1 Billion +

|+| No. Of travel sales online, U.S – 92.5 Billion USD

|+| 70% of Internet users search for information using a search engine

|+| 11% of the global internet users buy a product online every single day. That's 210+ million people EVERY SINGLE DAY!

Source : Plunkett research, Ltd

In other words, not having an Internet business presence today is detrimental to your financial health.

They say a year in the Internet business is like a dog year...equivalent to seven years in a regular person's life. In other words, it's evolving fast and faster.

Vinton Surf

Doing business on the Internet is going to be the norm in the days to come, and now is the time to position yourself accordingly.

I urge you not to skim or rush through this book, because by the time you are done with this training you will discover the numerous ways you can also have a piece of the "Internet business" pie in all fairness, and without stabbing anyone in the back!

The Internet has been the most fundamental change during my lifetime and for hundreds of years. Someone the other day said, *"It's the biggest thing since Gutenberg,"* and then someone else said *"No, it's the biggest thing since the invention of writing."* – Rupert Murdoch

You Are One Of The Lucky Ones
"I'm a great believer in luck, and I find the harder I work, the more I have of it" – Thomas Jefferson

The fact that you are going through this book makes you one of the lucky ones.

Yes...I really do mean it when I say you are lucky, and you are going to see why.

What makes you lucky? What do I mean by lucky?

You see, having luck is a notion that is misunderstood by many.

The common definition of luck is one that is usually given to someone who wins a lottery or something they never worked or asked for.

But part of my goal in training you to have a mindset of steel, to ensure you succeed online is to redefine popular notions such as luck.

First of all, let me start off by saying that **Luck is a competence**.

Yes…. A competence…

It is not a random, half-hazard or arbitrary concept.

Luck is a competence that can be worked on. You are responsible for the luck that comes your way.

Richard Essi

In other words, it simply means that you have the capacity to create luck in your environment by the daily actions you take.

"Luck is what happens when preparation meets opportunity"

And the action you are taking right now is part of those things that attracts luck – and this is irrespective of the person.

Having luck is activating the flow of opportunities.

Without opportunity, success can be every elusive, and in many cases close to impossible.

The more opportunities you have, the more you are likely to succeed.

With the right mindset, you will not only be able to recognize a golden opportunity, but you will also have the confidence to seize it.

Having a window of opportunity is what will allow you to radically change your circumstance.

Opportunities in your particular situation can be classified into three things:

1. Meeting the right people at the right time. The reason I work so hard on developing and maintaining a success mindset, and why I encourage you to do the same is simple:

"Birds of the same feather, flock together" – **Seneca**

In other words, success minded people tend to gravitate towards other success minded people, while negative and "victim-minded" people tend to attract each other.

"Don't wait for extraordinary opportunities. Seize common occasions

and make them great. Weak men wait for opportunities; strong men make them"

Case in point. Have you noticed how in most corporate or work environments there is always a group of people who complain about everything?

They gossip and complain about, the bosses, the working conditions, the salary, the weather, and sometimes everything under the sun!

These whiners and complainers tend to always flock together.

Then you have those who are always hanging out with the managers, staying a little late and coming in a little early, and who are always in an annoyingly "good mood" all the time. (I'm not talking about the fake and phony guys)

These guys just happen to be the ones that are promoted and people in general just seem to be attracted to their personality and charisma. Why is that?

Simple. These people have learnt the art of cultivating a success mindset, and the people that are drawn to them are like-minded people.

These same people seem to have all the "great" opportunities, and always seem to be at the right place, and at the right time. They are the lucky ones!

2. The Right timing. Being at the right place at the right time is what everybody wishes for.

But is it really something that can be left to the common definition of luck?

There is no such thing as being too old or too late to succeed.

Try and tell that to Harland David "Colonel Sanders" a 65 year veteran who took 100 USD and started Kentucky Fried Chicken.

3. Listening to the right demands. As an Internet entrepreneur, the trend has changed.

The old school way of developing and marketing a product was creating a product and inundating the market with your advertisement until the client finally bought your product.

Today, things have changed.

To increase the luck, and consequently increase the opportunity, you will need to listen to the market FIRST.

It is from your customer's expressed need, desire and problems that you will now design a product or service that is almost guaranteed to sell.

You need to be curious, and inquisitive.

Get out of your comfort zone.

If you keep doing the same thing over and over again, with the expectation of finding new opportunities, you will quickly wear yourself out and be discouraged.

Opportunity simply does not like routine. Period.

Opportunity tends to smile on people who network. Networking is not just about exchanging goods, services and ideas or even masterminding for that matter.

How To Think And Become A Successful Webpreneur

In my world, networking is all about having an address book with the primary objective of helping people connect.

It is where you match other people's needs and the solutions, FIRST.

In other words, having a network is creating a link between people. The best way to attain your objectives is to help others reach their objectives

"A wise man will make more opportunities than he finds" - Francis Bacon

Opportunity also smiles to people who know how to interpret failure.

Failure is like raw material. For those with the right mindset, failure is the raw material that is used to create astounding success.

So, if you stick to your dream of financial freedom and implement the principles I am sharing with you, and persevere on this track, you will definitely continue to increase your LUCK!

"A pessimist is one who makes difficulties of his opportunities and an optimist is one who makes opportunities of his difficulties" – Harry Truman

"Problems are only opportunities with thorns on them" - Hugh Miller

4 YOUR BODY IS YOUR SLAVE, NOT YOUR MASTER

"The body is an instrument, the mind its function, the witness and reward of its operation." - <u>George Santayana</u>

As you read earlier, my story so far has been one of self-discovery through the situations I have gone through and the places I have lived. Understanding that I have a body and a spirit, and that these two aspects of me are actually distinct, has greatly helped in stopping the self-sabotage that was going on within me.

For me, it's all about understanding what are the patterns that have shaped my life, my thinking system and consequently my decisions and choices.

Knowing yourself is doing an inventory of the gifts and talents you have as well as what you don't have.
Knowing the nature of your natural preferences wrapped up in your personality (the body) is the first step.
Understanding that there is a hierarchy between my body and my spirit tells me that my spirt (my will and true self) can be designed and redefined.

How To Think And Become A Successful Webpreneur

Your present thinking system no longer has to be defined by past emotional experiences or circumstances nor by the fears and anxieties of tomorrow.

How many times have you found yourself doing something you didn't want to do, or not doing something you wanted to do deep inside of you?

This tug of war between your mind and your body is as ancient as time.

The truth of the matter is that your mind which includes your will, and therefore your choices has always and will always be stronger than your body.

One of the main issues I have noticed over the years is how little emphasis is put on the importance of having the right mindset when embarking on this online entrepreneur journey.

I have seen, coached and observed good people with great intentions get clobbered by the sheer weight of the information they received without having the right tools to deal with this.

So, they end up delving into ALL this ocean of information only to drown.

You can see this by the amount books, courses, training dvds and the like gathering dust on the shelves, or gathering digital dust on the hard drives.

So you see, it is not so much about the program or tool you have, it is about YOU and what you think you are capable of.

Maybe that's something you can relate to. You keep looking for that simple blueprint of how to become a successful Internet Entrepreneur only to be presented with extremely complicated techniques using jargon that you barely understand, and after a couple of days or weeks of trial you quit.

The bottom line is this. Your body has its own will, but so does your mind. It is self destructive in its choices.

The good news is that your mind has always had the capacity to command your body.

You just need to provide it with the right instructions and it steer your body and your emotions in the right direction.

"Our limitations and success will be based, most often, on your own expectations for ourselves. What the mind dwells upon, the body acts upon." - Denis Waitley

Many people live life in general thinking that they are the ones making their own choices, not realizing that their bodies are the ones choosing absolutely everything for them.

They are slaves of their body and they don't even know it!

The body in general tends to choose what makes it feel good, but not necessarily what is good for it.

Here are a few examples of how to recognize a life led by the body rather than the mind :

|+| If your body could choose, it would eat as much food as it wanted, in unlimited quantities and whenever.

|+| Your body loves instant gratification and is never truly satisfied – there is always a need for more.

|+| Your body if left to decide will dictate how much sleep it needs, and there is no such thing as too much sleep

|+| Your body loves entertainment and pleasure, and is always looking for ways to indulge in more entertainment and pleasurable activities 24/7, EVERY SINGLE DAY

|+| Your body hates pain and discomfort, and will do everything to avoid this – It loves shortcuts

|+| Your body is selfish and thinks of only it's interests. It is centered on only what it will benefit.

|+| Your body "knows it all" and in unteachable and uncoachable, it does not like to be told what to do.

|+| Your body loves to reap the fruit of seeds it never sowed. In other words it hates effort but loves compensation

|+| Your body's mentality is programmed to autopreserve. It does not like anything that makes it look bad, or makes it step out of its comfort zone

You see, many people do not know this about themselves and they tend to give in to every demand made by the body.

The truth of the matter is that every successful entrepreneur that is worth mentioning has made the switch.

They have been able to inverse the tendency. They have at one time had to face the demands of the body, but have resisted and overcome the body to be master of their own bodies.

"In so far as the mind is stronger than the body, so are the ills contracted by the mind more severe than those contracted by the body." - Marcus Tullius Cicero

Professional athletes and artists will gladly share with you their experiences of how they are constantly having to deal with the demands of their body.

They will tell you how they have had to buffer themselves in order to acheive maximum peak performance.
Well, these same principles will apply to you. I want to not only push you to peak performance, but I want you to be fulfilled in doing so.

As a newbie on the net, you are going to be **distracted** by all kinds of flashy lights, all of which are very enticing and "urgent".

However, you will need to first condition your mind by giving it the tools it needs to navigate through this maze of information and opportunities screaming your name at every corner.

"Everything's in the mind. That's where it all starts. Knowing what you want is the first step toward getting it." - Mae West

The key to giving your mind the power to rule over your body is to feed it with the right information. It's almost like reading to your mind its bill of rights.

Your mind must know what **executive** power and **authority** is readily available to it.

So, rather than running off to buy the "latest secret/technique", think long term and realize that you are mostly the result of what and how you think.

It will even change what you buy.

Leaders don't buy the same products and services that followers do.

Just like the "success minded" focus and pay the price on things that the "lack minded" will consider too expensive futile or a waste of time.

It's really that simple!

I know this "positive mind" stuff can sometimes feel like it is futile and a waste of time.

I could agree with you to a certain extent, especially since there are a lot of bogus concepts that are packaged in gold wrappings out there.

Personally, I do not subscribe to a lot of those overly "new age" theories, but trust me… when you condition your mind accordingly it will make you endure and persevere.

How To Think And Become A Successful Webpreneur

Without endurance, determination and perseverance, you can kiss your financial freedom dreams an everlasting goodbye!

How to Guarantee Your Success by Investing in Yourself Today

"Reading is to the mind what exercise is to the body." - Joseph Addison

There Must be an Orientation Session

Do you still remember what orientation felt like on your first days of high school, college or even your first job?

It always felt a little overwhelming taking in all that information all at once right?

Let me explain further.

As soon as your enrollment is confirmed in a high school or university, there is what is commonly known as an orientation session.

The very reason for this orientation is to allow the students to not be overwhelmed by all the new information they are going to have to assimilate.

The same thing happens when you start a new job. Try to remember your first job or any new job after that.

There was always a general tour of what needed to be done (well, that was usually in the best of cases), where you would be seated, who you would be working with etc.

"As a single footstep will not make a path on the earth, so a single thought will not make a pathway in the mind. To make a deep physical path, we walk again and again. To make a deep mental path, we must think over and over the kind of thoughts we wish to dominate our lives." - Henry

Richard Essi

I also know that many of you probably didn't get as much training in the beginning of your new job as you would have liked, but you still managed to pull through right?

I know from experience that in most cases you would just find yourself thrown in there and asked to produce...right?

Well, this time around you get to call the shots on the duration of your orientation.

You get to decide how long you want this orientation to last.

Nevertheless, you don't want this orientation period to last too long otherwise, you will start getting overwhelmed.

So, what exactly should your orientation period look like?

Well, your orientation is more of a mind map of just having a general idea of where you are going.

You don't want to know all the details just yet, but you simply want to have an idea of what the journey entails.

You need some kind of written or mental plan.

For example, when you get on the highway, don't you want to know what exit to take beforehand?

Some people drive really fast, and others slowly, which means some might get to the exit faster than others, but knowing exactly which exit to take appeases the mind and allows you the driver to focus on the task at hand.

In this case, what you need to do is kind of glance through all of this book just to have an idea of what you will be covering – it consists of looking a little bit more in depth at the table of contents, so that you can do a mind map of where you are going.

It's always vital to know where you are going before you start.

If in your mind you are thinking that this is going to be a 200 meters race, then the kind of energy you will put in at the start will be different from one who thinks that the race is a 10 miles marathon.

Conditioning Your Mind Is The First Step
This is has got to be one of the most under looked and underestimated traits for many people looking to start an Internet Business.

Given the high failure rate of many newbie Web Entrepreneurs, I am amazed why not many talk about this.

Most people ask for a blueprint and a step by step program where they can simply implement and get the success they are so bent on having.

What I have realized however is that when these same people are given the step by step blueprint to follow, they are the same that get overwhelmed, and end up throwing in the towel because of the disappointment of the wrong expectations, because of the overwhelming amount of detailed information they are receiving.

"Effort only fully releases its reward after a person refuses to quit." – Napolean Hill

Those who have DECIDED to succeed eventually will.

Why is that?

Well, it's simply because they set their sight on a desired outcome, and they will not give up until they have achieved their objective.

They will keep pressing forward until they reach their stated goal.

"The empires of the future are the empires of the mind." - <u>Winston Churchill</u>

When you come to think about it, is always about attitude. If there is one thing I cannot stand it is people who abound in negativity.

Their outlook on life is always based on the bad things that "could" happen, but never about the good things that "could" also happen.

It's as if they are destined to have bad things happen to them, and when these bad things happen to them they almost feel comforted because it confirms what they have always been thinking deep inside of them.

I do not know of any successful entrepreneur that has started off wishing himself failure. Have they been faced with the most daunting and adverse situations? Absolutely!

However the successful entrepreneurs are the ones who say, I am going to make this thing work no matter what. It might take me 3 months or 3 years, but I WILL MAKE IT WORK!

That's the attitude.

"There are but two roads that lead to an important goal and to the doing of
great things: strength and perseverance." -Johann von Goethe

It is not so much about memorizing "The Power of Positive Thinking" by Dr. Norman Vincent Peale, but it is more about choosing to look at the harsh reality in the face, and STILL have hope.

You see, what usually happens is that people who embark on the positive thinking wagon without really considering the real meaning of what being positive means, tend to bury their head in the sand, and ignore all alarms going off and pretending they don't exist.

Having a positive attitude means looking at the alarms and at the potential crisis and responding with an attitude of looking for the opportunity in the crisis.

They say necessity is the mother of all invention right?

Well, if necessity is the mother of all inventions, it means that there was a breed of entrepreneurs who saw crisis, and necessity as something that stimulated their creative juices, and that is how 95% of the appliances and technologies we use today were created.

They could have cried doom, but they decided to seize the opportunity that was being presented to them in the form of crisis.

A positive mental outlook means turning "lemon-like" situations into "lemonade". That would mean recognizing that the lemon is bitter. Ignoring the fact that lemon is bitter is foolish, because it is, whether you acknowledge it or not.

It is what you do with the bitterness of the lemon that makes the difference.

"I do not think there is any other quality so essential to success of any kind, as the quality of perseverance. It overcomes everything...even nature" - John D. Rockefeller

So you are going to have to treat this Internet business of yours like a REAL business. Don't say things like "*I want to try out this Internet Business thing to see if it really works*".

No, please don't say things like that, because if you do that, you would have failed before even trying.

You don't try to be successful you choose to become successful!

"Be miserable. Or motivate yourself. Whatever has to be done, it's always your choice." - <u>Wayne Dyer</u>

Muse on the fact that this is going to be your new profession.

Treat it as your Bachelor or Masters degree, treat it like a new high paying job where you will have to fly on your own soon.

Put some positive pressure on yourself.

Don't try to do this after having gone to the bathroom, or after a snack, or after a short nap or after a quick cleaning of the house etc....all these type of "justifiable" excuses are nothing but time wasters, and productivity killers.

They don't want you to take action NOW! They want you to procrastinate until you end up being overwhelmed by all that needs to be done.

"Procrastination is one of the most common and deadliest of diseases, and its toll on success and happiness is heavy" - Wayne Gretzky

I am taking the time to really explore this point, because most people tend to say, so when will you reveal the hidden code on how to run my Internet Business?

When do I take the blue pill?

So, what is the magic formula?

Well, first of all, there is no hidden code.

There is no "blue pill", and there is no magic formula.

That is definitely not what you are going to get in this book, but you are getting the "meat and bones", the "armor", the "architecture" you need to build a 6-7 figure Internet business empire.

How To Think And Become A Successful Webpreneur

"No great thing is created suddenly." - Epictetus

This book like I mentioned before is a compilation of wisdom learnt from my numerous success and failures, as well as from some of my friends and partners, and when we actually compared notes with the process of some our mentors and coaches, we realized that they all had these traits.

Every wealthy and successful entrepreneur once started out with nothing but a passionate idea.

They all went through feelings of incompetence, but they continued working on their incompetencies by making mistakes and acquiring more and more skill through books and systems like the one you are currently studying.

They eventually reached a point where they were so competent that they did not even realize it anymore – it had now become normal for them.

"You always do what you want to do. This is true with every act. You may say that you had to do something, or that you were forced to, but actually, whatever you do, you do by choice. Only you have the power to choose for yourself." - W. Clement Stone

I want you to take a real close look at the diagram that is explained in the link below:

http://www.businessballs.com/consciouscompetencelearningmodel.ht m

The diagram illustrated there applies to every development phase.

From child to adult, from student to teacher, from newbie to expert, from rookie to professional etc.

It is a cycle that everyone goes through in life.

It is important to understand the cycle shown in the diagram stated in the above link because it clearly shows that when followed properly, you will eventually attain a place of unconscious incompetence which is where your skills and knowledge are now worth quite a bit, and it is now up to you to determine how you want to monetize this.

"By stretching yourself beyond your perceived level of confidence, you accelerate your development of competence" - Michael J. Gelb

In other words, what will happen or what has already happened is that you get excited about the opportunity of working from home via the Internet.

You can see the potential of making a full time income and more from the sheer power of the access you now have to a global market.

"He who would learn to fly one day must first learn to stand and walk and run and climb and dance; one cannot fly into flying." - Friedrich Nietzsche

However, as you continue inquiring and researching on the matter, you begin to realize that you are completely ignorant on the matter.

You start to realize that this thing is not as easy as it appeared.

You get so overwhelmed by the information that you start doubting if this is something you can actually do...it's all beginning to sound a little too complicated for someone like you who has barely enough time to sleep!

And this is unfortunately where most people quit.

But if you can go through the pain of working and honing your skills then you will realize that there is truly no gain without pain!

"Whenever you make a mistake or get knocked down by life, don't look back at it too long. Mistakes are life's way of teaching you. Your capacity for occasional blunders is inseperable from your capacity to reach your goals. No one wins them all, and all your failures, when they happen are just part of your growth. Shake off your blunders. How will you know your

limits without an occasional failure? Never quit. Your turn will come" - Og Mandino

If you are reading this book, then you are already in phase two where you have realized that you lack the specialized mindset skill and knowledge to build and run a successful Internet Business, and you are therefore looking to hone that skill...correct?

Without even realizing it, you have done two things that characterize 90% of entrepreneurs, which are taking action, and choosing to invest in your education.

You have decided to break through the barrier of discomfort and ignorance.

You now understand that people buy from people they know like and trust.

So, in educating yourself and learning to train your mind to think and act like a leader, you have decided to position yourself in such a way that people can know you, like you and trust you.

This takes work, soul searching and total conviction. Once all these things are aligned, your journey is 75% complete.

"Adopt the pace of nature: her secret is patience." - **Ralph Waldo Emerson**

Don't try to know everything at once, just mind map the path you are going to take to get to your destination, and follow your daily and weekly goals, and you will find the journey refreshing and enriching.

"We rate ability in men by what they finish, not by what they begin." - Anonymous

"The road to success is dotted with many tempting parking places" - Anonymous

Richard Essi

"The greatest oak was once a little nut who held its ground" - **Anonymous**

"He conquers who endures" - **Persius**

"You can't go through life quitting everything. If you're going to achieve anything, you've got to stick to something" – **Family Matters**

"It's not that I'm so smart, it's just that I stay with problems longer." - **Albert Einstein**

"Problems are not stop signs, they are guidelines" - **Robert Schuller**

"Our greatest glory is not in never failing, but in rising up every time we fail" – **Ralph Waldo Emerson**

"Many of the great achievements of the world were accomplished by tired and discouraged men who kept on working" - **Anonymous**

"Age wrinkles the body, quitting wrinkles the soul" - **Anonymous**

"Nothing in this world can take the place of persistence. Talent will not ; nothing is more common than unsuccessful people with talent. Genius will not ; unrewarded genius is almost a proverb. Education will not ; the world is full of educated derelicts. Persistence and determination alone are omnipotent. The slogan 'press on' has solved and always will solve the problems of the human race" - **Calvin Coolidge**

"Edison failed 10,000 times before he made the electric light. Do not be discouraged if you fail a few times." - **Napolean Hill**

5 WHO ARE YOU AND WHAT IS YOUR PURPOSE?

The Ethics of Success - The Real Key to Unlimited Wealth

The ethics of success speaks of the intangible traits that you will find in the majority of successful Internet entrepreneurs or many entrepreneurs for that matter.

It is those things that they possess that you cannot touch or feel that allow them to turn into gold everything they touch.

It is that thing that gives them the confidence that no matter what happens to them, they know how start all over again and always achieve the same level of success.

"I write because something inner and unconscious forces me to. That is the first compulsion. The second is one of ethical and moral duty. I feel responsible to tell stories that inspire readers to consider more deeply who they are." - David Guterson

The ethics of success speaks of the mindset, the habits, the philosophy and the motivation behind everything that is done.

In other words, if you really set out to help your customers and partners, then you take the focus off you and in doing so, you are sowing seeds of appreciation and gratitude in the person you are trying to help.

The principle of doing to others what you would like done to you, is true beyond your religious beliefs. It is one of those things that are built into life itself, in the same way that you cannot see, touch or smell air. So, not only is it there, but it is indispensable for your survival on this earth.

Most people get online with a "quick buck" mentality.

Basically they are looking for ways to make money as fast as possible, and they don't really care if in the process they will destroy the dreams of many. They are desperate and they need money now.

So, when they finally "succeed" in finding other desperate and gullible people like them, then they turn around and sell their story to a bunch of other desperate Internet Entrepreneurs, and the cycle continues without end.

For me that is the "get rich or die tryin'" mentality, and I do not subscribe to that. You could make money that way, and that would be your choice, but that is not my philosophy.

"If you don't have integrity, you have nothing. You can't buy it. You can have all the money in the world, but if you are not a moral and ethical person, you really have nothing." - Henry Kravis

Based on all what I have seen in my 36 years on this earth and from the wisdom I have learnt from dozens of mentors, six figure earners, millionaires, spiritual leaders and wise men, I have discovered that wealth is not just about money.
Wealth is complete package in which money is included. It is a life package that contains the joy, the peace that money alone cannot give. It also contains the satisfaction of living a purposeful life and the

comprehension that having a legacy is like having a blank check for yourself and for your children.

"Wealth, like happiness, is never attained when sought after directly. It comes as a by-product of providing a useful service." - <u>Henry Ford</u>

Discovering your Purpose and Living Your Life According to Your Calling

"Success demands singleness of purpose." - <u>Vince Lombardi</u>

Let me start off by asking you this question. If money and time was not an issue what would you like to be doing? What would you do for free without pay?

You don't have to be the first to invent something in order for you to feel like you have a purpose or meaning in this life.

It's easy to feel like a number in the crowd, but is it really true? Some people feel comfortable being a number in the crowd, and that's OK.

However, if you are reading this book today, then you are probably one of those who dares to go against the crowd, and against the status quo!

"When I chased after money, I never had enough. When I got my life on purpose and focused on giving of myself and everything that arrived into my life, then I was prosperous." - <u>Wayne Dyer</u>

Well, believe it or not, there are not many like you.
You don't realize this, but you have just made it to the top 5% crowd of successful Internet entrepreneurs, and here's why.

Almost everybody wishes for something, but they are not really sure they want it.

You, on the other hand, you want something more out of this life, and you are therefore ready to take the required action to get what you want, this is what makes you completely different from the crowd around you where all you hear is whining!

"An ounce of action is worth a ton of theory." - <u>Ralph Waldo Emerson</u>

You are unique.

No other person here on earth has your exact same fingerprints. You have your own voice, your own perspective on things, and you need to find an outlet or a venue to express this.

The Internet just serves as a global audience.

Maybe there is something that you absolutely love and you are passionate about, but don't have the skill for it...what are you waiting for? Acquire the skill and deliver us from all the homogeneity and copy cats out there, and release your creativity and originality in this pre-formatted world of ours.

I remember a friend of mine in University, Lisa.

Lisa could not sing even if her life depended on it, but she absolutely loved music, especially R-n-B. She knew the humble beginnings of many of the famous artist at the time and she had already identified them as future international stars.

You see, Lisa had an ear for up and coming R-n-B artists. When she heard someone sing, she knew immediately if this person was gifted and had the opportunity to make it or not.

How To Think And Become A Successful Webpreneur

To make a long story short, Lisa ended up moving from Chicago to Atlanta to start a new career in the music industry. The last I heard Lisa was an integral part of a popular record label, and she has an Internet Strategy where she scouts and identifies talent via online videos and podcast sites.

"A real decision is measured by the fact that you've taken a new action. If there's no action, you haven't truly decided." - Tony Robbins

I was talking to yet another friend of mine Sophie.
Sophie is a gifted African food cook. She can cook the most exotic and tasteful African dishes. She tried doing some catering but realized that it was simply too costly and too demanding for a one woman show.
Today, Sophie has compiled a bunch African food recipes that she will soon be making available in course where she will have all her recipes as well as all the step-by-step "how to" videos on how to make the most amazing exotic dishes and wow your friends and family.

I could go on and on, but I think you get my point. What do you hate? What irritates you? What do you like? What can't you live without? What are you passionate about? What are you scared of?

All these things will give you an indication of what you could do to express your own voice without feeling like you are copying someone else….it's impossible anyway because you are unique.

Think about musicians.

There are millions of musicians out there and they all have an audience!

In some cases, some musicians take a popular song and just re-sing it with their own spin on it, and it works!

So, don't limit yourself by saying "oh…someone is already doing it".

Know instead that nobody else can do it like you! What you are doing will significantly impact your own life and the lives of thousands, if not millions for the best.

Don't just try….give your everything!

"You are unique, and if that is not fulfilled, then something has been lost."
- <u>Martha Graham</u>

6 BECOMING A SUCCESSFUL ENTREPRENEUR IS A CHOICE

Your Habits will Determine Your Financial Success and its Duration

"We first make our habits, and then our habits make us." - <u>John Dryden</u>

Have you ever heard of the **Pygmalion Effect**?

The Pygmalion Effect: The Pygmalion effect is a theory that was discovered and propagated by Rosenthal and Jacobsen in the late 60's. It was a theory that was developed in a teacher student context, but which remains even more applicable to all spheres of life.

Basically, Rosenthal and Jacobsen concluded that teacher expectations influenced student performance. So, a positive expectation on a student would influence the student's performance positively, while a negative expectation would influence a student's performance negatively.

In other words, this phenomenon described as the Pygmalion effect is a form of self-fulfilling prophecy where people who internalize their negative belief system tend to manifest and experience the exact same things, in the same way that people who internalize their positive belief system seem to manifest and experience the exact same things. It is the universal law of sowing and reaping that is at work.

So, if we expect certain behaviors from ourselves then we are more likely to to act in ways that will cause this expected behavior even more likely to occur.

So, if you are lazy, undisciplined, uncoachable and proud, and you know you are like that, then you probably don't think to highly of yourself, and you have some set expectations based on these character traits.

"Not managing your time and making excuses are two bad habits. Don't put them both together by claiming you "don't have the time." - Bo Bennett

But what if you could change your character by changing your habits?

Remember your personality will always be the same, but your character can change. If you change your character and start becoming more accountable, disciplined, hard working, early riser, humble, coachable, I can almost guarantee that the expectations you have for yourself will radically change, and as such your outcome will also change.

You see, habits are like rail tracks. Once you build them right, you are pretty much guaranteed to arrive at destination. So, if we can change our habits, we can raise our success belief system, and consequently we will also change our outcome.

"I never could have done what I have done without the habits of punctuality, order, and diligence, without the determination to concentrate myself on one subject at a time." - Charles Dickens

How To Think And Become A Successful Webpreneur

There are many proverbs and wise sayings that talk about the power of habits.

There is one in particular that I like that states that doing the same thing over and over again and expecting a different result is the very definition of insanity.

So, maybe you have been wishing for quite some time to start an Internet business, and to really break free from your 9-5 rut, and the last time you checked you were still working in your 9-5 job and this for the last 5 years.

If this is your case or similar then you have a habit problem. You may have a strong want or desire to succeed and charge on to financial freedom, but if you don't build the right boat or place the right tracks, you may start.....but you will never finish!

"Habits are safer than rules; you don't have to watch them. And you don't have to keep them either. They keep you." - <u>Frank Crane</u>

Habits are long term. They will allow you to keep keeping on when the going gets tough. There will be times when your body, your emotions even your desire will at their all time low. The only thing that will keep this train of yours moving is the rail road tracks. You won't feel every time that you slow down that you have to start from scratch. There will be a sense of continuity in your movement.

There is nothing more discouraging than starting and then stopping, and then starting all over again, and then stopping. Build your railroad tracks through solid and effective habits, and watch your outcome change because of a new expectation level:

How do we make change? Well, either we change our beliefs or our actions, only then can we shift the cycle.

So, How Long does it take to Form or Create a Habit?
A habit is defined in the dictionary as:

a. A recurrent, often unconscious pattern of behavior that is acquired through frequent repetition.

b. An established disposition of the mind or character

In plain terms, a habit can be described as a reflexive and repetitive behavior.

A habit is either good or bad depending on your moral values. Usually, the things we do the most naturally every single day are actually a sum of habits. For example, I used to have this habit of having "my morning coffee" before I started any sort of work. I believe this habit is still shared by 80% of people. Others have the habit of jogging in the morning before going to work, or going to the gym at noon or after work.

In fact, research has proven that there is a two way relationship between our conscious actions and our unconscious actions. In other words, the habits we create become automatic reflexes over a period of time – they become the things we do unconsciously.

"In order to change unwanted habits and actions, it is important to take the time to get to know yourself." - Darren L. Johnson

Depending on the type of habit you want to create it will either take a slight effort or a massive effort to create. Maybe, all that is required is that you work on a certain part of your business every single day. Maybe it's going to be about creating more value for your business, or maybe it's going to be about calling, e-mailing and following up on your clients.

How To Think And Become A Successful Webpreneur

The bottom line is that the more you perform these "chores" or repetitive actions, the more automated they become.

Habits are extremely powerful. These are the real secrets of the most successful. Think about it....if you see a spectacular weight loss in someone, I can almost guarantee that there is a spectacular habit that was developed to achieve those kinds of results.

Habits are like wild beasts. If you create and manage them they will do your bidding and take you to places you've only dreamt of, but if the habits take on a life of their own, they will not only control you, but they will destroy you !

So, getting back to the question at hand. How long does it take to form a new habit? Well, I am not sure that there is a written formula for this, but based on my interviews and my research, I would say between 4-6 weeks.

But if you would really like to make that habit stick for like glue, then you might want to add another 2-3 weeks.

Remember we are talking about creating habits that are directly linked to your activity as an Internet Entrepreneur, so this is very specific to our field.

You see, wishful thinking will not get you to where you want to be. You can read all the testimonials you want, you can know the names of all your mentors and even quote them on occasion, but what will make you capable of having their kind of success, is your ability to imitate what they do. You need to understand and integrate the unseen dynamics behind the outward "success" you see.

I remember a story Jake, a multi-millionaire once said. He was recounting the story of how a young gentleman by the name of Sam had come up to him.

Here is how it played out. It is Sam who ran up to get a glimpse of his hero:

"Hi Jake! I am so excited to see you!"

Sam continued by making the following statement:

"Wow! I really love how you have succeed Jake! Your rags-to-riches story is truly inspiring! I wish there was a way for you to just lay hands on me and give me the success you now have."

To this Jake replied:

"Young man, what's your name?"

When Sam had given him his name here is what Jake the millionaire said:

"Sam, it's really nice to meet you, and I am really glad that my story inspired you. I really hope it will inspire you to action. You see Sam, even if I were to lay hands on you and give you all the success I currently have, do you realize that you would also have to receive all the rags, pain, betrayal frustration, discouragement, fear, and tears that created this success? They are one and the same coin you know!"

Jake says that Sam had smiled politely, thanked him and left.

Personally, I am really curious to know what kind of questions were ignited in his mind after Jake's response. He must have been asking himself a million questions.

To desire a successful online business is one thing, but to bring that desire to manifestation you are going to need consistent targeted actions over a long period of time, this is how habits are created, **because habit has the birthing power that desire does not.**

If for example, you have been living with a strong desire to exit the rat race in your corporate environment for the last couple of years, and you still have not been able to walk away, then it is not that you don't know how or what to do, it is just that you have not stuck with one thing long enough to make it work.

How To Think And Become A Successful Webpreneur

Your desires and wishes have been betrayed by wrong patterns and habits. It is your daily routine and habits that will determine your level of success.

Again, patterns and habits are like train tracks....once you place them, all kinds of trains and all at different speeds can ride through.

"Successful people are simply those with successful habits." - <u>Brian Tracy</u>

7 WHY CONVICTION ALWAYS BEATS OBLIGATION

Why Conviction Beats Obligation – Hands Down!

"Being the richest man in the cemetery doesn't matter to me. Going to bed at night saying we've done something wonderful, that's what matters to me." - Steve Jobs

"A 'No' uttered from the deepest conviction is better than a 'Yes' merely uttered to please, or worse, to avoid trouble." - Mohandas Gandhi

YOU and YOU Alone are Responsible for Your Life – You are Not a Victim

This is probably the point that should be on the very top of your traits.

All successful entrepreneurs both offline and online understand this point very clearly. All these entrepreneurs have learnt to make the most of what life has served them. I

f life has given you what you describe as « lemon » circumstances then make some lemon juice out of that. If you feel like you have bad apples in your life, then turn those bad apples into jam, apple pie or something of the sort. It is never about what happened or what is happening to you right now, it is more about how you respond.

"Every great man, every successful man, no matter what the field of endeavor, has known the magic that lies in these words: every adversity has the seed of an equivalent or greater benefit." - W. Clement Stone

Nick Vujicic (I will make several references to this amazing man) is a young gentleman who was born without arms and without legs.

Now, here's a guy who had all the reasons to curse life and God and just die! But he didn't do that!
Instead, he has spent his entire life inspiring millions around the globe, and he has sown seeds of hope, belief and determination in the lives of people who have everything he doesn't have. Today, Nick is an accomplished entrepreneur with true wealth!

No matter the proof you may have about the injustice you are facing in your life today, be it racial, financial, professional, relational etc. you simply cannot continue to sing the same blaming song all the time.

You need to know that wherever it is you want to be in your Internet business in the next 1-3 years is directly linked to the choices and decisions you make today. Integrate this, and the sky will be the limit to how high you will soar!

"Never be bullied into silence. Never allow yourself to be made a victim. Accept no one's definition of your life; define yourself." - Harvey Fierstein

Maybe you feel like you are not like the popular or fortunate type that has connections, knows people and has the gift of gab. Maybe you have had to fight for everything you have had this far, maybe things have not come to you easily.

61

Maybe you have had to implode in many situations because you did not have the luxury to explode! Well, all these circumstances have built your character. You do not take anything for granted.

It's like what I told you about my story earlier. Arriving to the States from a third world country was not only a culture shock, but it was also a realization of how lucky and privileged I was to be able to have all these numerous opportunities available to me.

This is definitely different from the average kid born in the western world who has more than 35 different cereals to choose from, and so many different clothes to choose from that it becomes a real problem to know what to wear on a given day of the week.

I recommend that you take another look at the things you have gone through or are currently going through in trying to create a better life for yourself. What you will notice is the following:

|+| **You are very realistic**. You know what the challenges are, and you also know what needs to be done to overcome these challenges. You are definitely not naive or ignorant

|+| **Resilience and determination has been built inside of you**. With all the rejections, injustices, and difficulties that life has thrown at you, you keep getting back up. You know what it feels to be knocked down, but you also know the essence of getting back up. This resiliency is what makes you successful even before arriving at your specific monetary or lifestyle goal.

|+| **You are a self starter**. In other words, you are your best motivator. Because of all that you have been through, you have all the necessary fuel and energy to push things forward.

|+| **You are an Independent thinker**. You are free to do things your own way, because you are not part of the crowd. Your circumstances have not been like the majority.

|+| **You are compassionate**. The harshness of the blows you have received has created a certain kind of sensitivity and real care in you. Your products and services will reflect this aspect of you, and you will also approach your clients with this perfume, and it will be like a breath of fresh air in a world where compassion and sensitivity are serious underdogs!

|+| **You understand the power of humility**. You understand that pride always comes before the fall. Doing business online with others will require that you connect with many people. Connecting with people with the utmost humility causes people to trust you. Trust is a currency online that you cannot afford to not have. Honesty, humility and Integrity are now values that will translate into true wealth for you in your Internet business

You Have Clear Goals and You Know Exactly what You Want

There is a question I love asking my mentees and my audience. The question is: What is it you want to achieve and where do you see yourself 5 years from now?

I am always amazed at how this question creates an immediate silence or puzzled and confused facial expressions.

Why is that?

Simple, people are so busy treading the mill that they have really not taken the time to sit down and evaluate where they are and where they are going. They are more in survival mode than they are in thinking mode.

"Dream small dreams. If you make them too big, you get overwhelmed and you don't do anything. If you make small goals and accomplish them, it gives you the confidence to go on to higher goals." - <u>John H. Johnson</u>

"Goals help you channel your energy into action." - <u>Les Brown</u>

Consider Amy and her husband Greg.

Amy works two jobs. Once as a nurse and the other as a baby sitter, so basically she is up most nights doing her shift as a nurse, and she is up most of the day doing babysitting.

Amy has two teenage kids, and her hands are full. Greg her husband, is an IT guy who is always on call and who works long hours in support, and can never really commit to a weekend because his phone or beeper could go off any time.

When you talk to Greg and Amy about what their goals are, and where they want to be 5 years from now, they might actually be offended! Their primary concern is surviving! If there is anything they want, it is a break from all the running and the stress. They want to spend time together as a couple and as a family. That is their immediate goal.

It is people like Greg and Amy who need to make it a priority to force a break in time to plan and set some specific financial goals. They need to make a time limited goal, break the goal into actionable steps and simply take massive action. This is what awaits you in the second part of this book.

If you were to drive to a new city, one that you have never been to and know very little about, do you think you would need a map or a GPS? I am Sure you would!

Could you make it without a map to a specific destination? You probably could, but how many gas station stops for directions would you have to make before arriving at your destination.

How much gas would it cost getting approximate directions, getting lost, and how much time would you lose? You need a clear plan. You need step-by-step directives to get to where you want.

How To Think And Become A Successful Webpreneur

"Goals provide the energy source that powers our lives. One of the best ways we can get the most from the energy we have is to focus it. That is what goals can do for us; concentrate our energy." - <u>Denis Waitley</u>

You Understand the Power of Focus

"That's been one of my mantras - focus and simplicity. Simple can be harder than complex: You have to work hard to get your thinking clean to make it simple. But it's worth it in the end because once you get there, you can move mountains." - Steve Jobs

They say focused energy is one of the strongest forms of energy in the world. In other words when you take any kind of form of energy, be it light, water or wind, you will discover power beyond explanation. Think about it.

Light on its own is simply light. It is the opposite of darkness, and it helps you see. But when you take these same light rays and you concentrate that light energy, you end up with laser, solar panels etc. What about water? Water in itself is as innocent as can be. You need it to drink, and to bathe. Basically it is a human necessity. However, if you take a concentrated quantity or surface area of water, you can produce millions of volts of electricity.

Concentrated or focused human energy can also produce some spectacular results. I mean, we see this with our kids and sometimes with us. It could be in education, sports or whatever. The moment we are able to focus our energy on one particular activity, we end up innovating.

"Most people have no idea of the giant capacity we can immediately command when we focus all of our resources on mastering a single area of our lives." - <u>Tony Robbins</u>

Your undivided focus will mean turning every distraction off. If you want to produce some spectacular financial results in your Internet business then you cannot afford to start and run your business with the TV in the background. Every day you will be assaulted by all kinds of distractions. Here are a few examples:

1. Your emotions and feelings. Yes, these can be distractions too! Your feelings are always unpredictable. Today you feel like it, tomorrow you don't...

2. Disappointments. The world will not stop because you are trying to start and run an Internet business. Things will not always go as planned. Life will continue to put demands on you, so you need to manage your disappointments and not let them interfere with your focused activities

3. Other responsibilities. This is where you will have to develop complexity in your character. Multitasking is not a skill limited to computers and certain job descriptions, it is a skill you must possess if you are going to be a successful Internet Entrepreneur. You need to be able to shift your focus accordingly and in the right order of priorities.

4. Other opportunities. They say the grass is always greener on the other side. Whenever you start any kind of business online, you will almost immediately be bombarded with other business opportunities. You will be tempted to buy into these opportunities for a later date. Don't do it! If if is not a tool or something that can help your business TODAY, don't buy it.

The Internet is also referred to as the World Wide Web. That's the meaning of the "www" you type in front of every website you visit. This simply means that to work on the Internet requires extreme focus, if not you will easily get caught up in the "web" of distractions, and you will waste time, effort and money trying to get back to the center of things.

"Focus is a matter of deciding what things you're not going to do." - <u>John Carmack</u>

How To Think And Become A Successful Webpreneur

You are an Authentic Giver

"We make a living by what we get, but we make a life by what we give." - Winston Churchill

Being an authentic giver simply means that in your core philosophy as an Internet Entrepreneur, you want to add real value to your customers. This means that you are not looking to make a "quick buck" off your customers.

In other words, at the core of your value system, you understand that it is better to give than to receive. You know that the way you treat and value your customer will determine the level of credibility you will have in the eyes of your customer. Credibility and trust on the Internet translates to massive profits.

The same sales principles that apply offline are valid online. For example, every customer was once a potential customer. What made him transition to being a customer, was because he got to know, like and trust the sales guy.

People like to interact with people they know like and trust right? Well, many forget that the customers that interact with them are not just credit card numbers. They are **real** people with **real** families and **real** needs and they are looking for **real** customized solutions for their situation.

Customers can sense a "phony" a mile away. So if you are going to sell by using hype, it might work for the first or two occasions, and you might make quite a bit of money, but in the long run your credibility will diminish and if you kill your credibility online, you might as well close shop.

If you are offering a particular service or product in your field, become the go-to expert for this. It is your expertise that will give you that authoritative voice, where your opinion will count for something.

All successful entrepreneurs have understood this, that is why they become professional at what they do.

Remember what we said earlier, this is not a hobby, this is not about "trying it out" to see if it works.

Strive to be the best in your field, and give without reserve and see how the seeds of giving you sow will turn into a harvest beyond your wildest imagination.

"It is the service we are not obliged to give that people value most." - James Cash Penney

You Understand the Power of "NOW"

"One today is worth two tomorrows." - Benjamin Franklin

There is no greater dream killer than procrastination. All successful people have learnt to deal with this giant. Yes, it is a giant! What makes this particular dream killer powerful is that it is very subtle. It is present in nearly all areas of our lives.

In lay man terms, to procrastinate is to do tomorrow what you could have done today. You need to be energetic and passionate, you need to understand the power of time, and momentum. There is no such thing as the perfect moment. This is something that my wife and I discovered before we started having kids.

We were always waiting for that perfect financial situation in order to have kids....the problem was, it never felt like the right moment. It is only when we finally decided to act without seeing the « how » that things started changing for us.

We were living in a tiny studio. We wanted to change apartments first before having kids, and that is what we were waiting for. It was not until we decided to go for it, that an opportunity to have a bigger apartment opened up for us.

There is no better time than now. There is no better time than today. Your tomorrow is all about the actions you take today.

It's good to think things through, but if the thinking does not produce a concrete action, then your thinking would have simply wasted you time, and when doing business online, you cannot afford to be paralyzed by every detail.

If not you will fall into a very popular online disease called Information overload! This disease will paralyze you and kill your business.

"You see, it's never the environment; it's never the events of our lives, but the meaning we attach to the events - how we interpret them - that shapes who we are today and who we'll become tomorrow." - <u>Tony Robbins</u>

8 DISCOVER THE REAL POWER OF ENTHUSIASM

"Enthusiasm is excitement with inspiration, motivation, and a pinch of creativity." - <u>Bo Bennett</u>

So, what exactly is Enthusiasm, and how will this add to your bottom line?

Enthusiasm is that feeling you get when you are excited about an idea, a person, an event or something of the like.

It is a surge of energy that emerges as a result of the excitement and the emotional charge that this idea or interest generates.

The good thing about enthusiasm is that it puts you in an emotional peak state. Being in that state is what makes you move mountains. When people are depressed their enthusiasm levels are low, but when they are excited and happy about something, their enthusiasm levels are high.

Enthusiasm generally equates to massive action.

Have you ever talked to a teenager who is about to or just bought his/her new dream car? Their enthusiasm is contagious. Their energy has no limits, he/she will wash their car 3 times a day just to keep it nice and shiny.

How To Think And Become A Successful Webpreneur

What about a young adult who is madly in love with his soon to be wife? Have you seen the hurdles he is willing to jump over just to woo this girl? There is no mountain too high for him to climb in order to woo his beloved!

You will discover that people who are enthusiastic spread good cheer and optimism all around them, simply because enthusiasm is contagious.

So, if we are going to embark on a financial freedom journey – one that is mostly uphill, then we are going to need plenty of enthusiasm.

"Enthusiasm... the sustaining power of all great action." - Samuel Smiles

Are You Enthusiastic about Being an Employee Or A Webpreneur?

The idea of walking away from a 9-5 job and telling your boss to go fly a kite was surveyed as one the top 5 fantasies of most employees. So this is clearly something that many employees think about. There are even commercials that entertain these fantasies by showing employees doing all kinds of crazy things in the office and to their "horrible bosses" before leaving the job after a lottery winning.

However, we are not talking about winning the lottery (which has proven to be quite detrimental in most cases), we are talking about building a real Internet business that will outlast you and hopefully your children.

Getting up, and "rushing" through traffic to get to work can become a mindless habit that will eventually make you numb over a given period of time. Most people try to kill this monotony by changing jobs, taking different routes to work, or trying to switch things up a little bit.

The majority of employees that have Internet access at work admit spending an average of 10 hours per week on non work related websites.

So, let's imagine that you are one of those employees. What would that mean then if you were one of those people? What if you actually started surfing and looking for an Internet business while at work? Either way, your surfing and searching was done in parallel with your "real job", so the reality is that in the back of your mind, surfing, researching on the Internet is not really a "real job".

You probably don't think of this consciously, but unconsciously there is something that does not register an Internet business as a "real job". Do you know how to test this? Try to envisage how you will react at the next Easter, Thanksgiving or Christmas family gathering, and how you will respond when someone will ask you what you are now doing (assuming you are now full time in your Internet business).

So, when asked the question about what you do, are you going to stammer, try to justify and over explain or are you going to confidently say that you an Internet Entrepreneur who runs a business online?

If you can answer this question comfortably, then you are already half way there. If you are not able to answer this question comfortably, then don't worry, you have just identified a thinking habit/pattern that you will need to evaluate, break, and replace.

So now that you have identified the "Job" mentality which is usually one where you are told what to do, you are going to now have to create a new one. Now you are the boss and at the same time the employee. Yes, that's right the boss AND the employee. You need to see the big picture, devise the plan, and then execute it.

In a work setting, you usually sit down with your boss and you go over your objectives together. This time around, you are going to be the one drafting your very own objectives, and you will be the one establishing the time frames and the due dates. So, you will need to be extremely clear on where you are going and what you need to do to get there.

How To Think And Become A Successful Webpreneur

If you don't feel like you have the entrepreneur mentality, don't worry because all mentalities can be created by something you now know very well – habits!

Going from employee to entrepreneur is not only about what you do, it is more about how you think, and that is why we are taking the time to really craft your every thought, so that all your actions will be executed on a solid entrepreneur mentality that will serve as your foundation.

"Enthusiasm is the yeast that makes your hopes shine to the stars. Enthusiasm is the sparkle in your eyes, the swing in your gait. The grip of your hand, the irresistible surge of will and energy to execute your ideas." HenryFord

9 INTEGRITY VS. MANIPULATION

Not Everything that Glitters is Gold

This is the rule of thumb for every newbie Internet Entrepreneur. This is where most newbies fall flat on their faces. The lights and glitter are enticing, but it's nothing more than great packaging – the content is a whole different story.

If you are going to be offering services or information products (e-books, videos, audios), then you are going to see a lot of hype! You will see plenty of bold claims about tools and solutions for newbie Internet Entrepreneurs like you. In fact there is a huge multi-million dollar market for new Internet Entrepreneur looking to start and run their business using the Internet. So, just so you know, you are going to be swimming in an ocean filled with great white sharks!

No need to worry though, I will help you survive in this dog eat dog jungle. Why am I so confident about this? Well, that's because I have been one of their favorite type of prey. I have forked out tens and tens of thousands on different products looking for that particular push button miraculous solution that they keep dangling in front of me.

I have been a sales letter junkie. In other words, I have fallen for nearly every product that has been sold with some of these amazing and convincing sales letters.

How To Think And Become A Successful Webpreneur

These letters are like cash sucking machines. They know how to press the right emotional buttons in you, and before you know it, you are buying not one product, but all the products – even those you didn't need.

Let me give you a typical scenario that I have experienced one too many times.

When I first started off on the Internet to really seriously start a business on the Internet, I had some money to spare like any normal entrepreneur that wants to start a business.

The only difference was that I didn't have tens of thousands like it would have been required in an offline or brick and mortar business. No, I simply had a few thousands, for the market research, product development and the initial marketing.

I had a few ideas in mind, and I was already starting to work on those ideas. In the meantime I kept trying to map out strategy. I wanted to understand how my sales funnel was going to flow, what would be the price of my products. Where could I find the kind of targeted traffic that I needed to really take my business to another level.

So, I had identified that I needed help in keyword research (keywords being the words people type in Google to search for what they want), product development and traffic. So, I found myself having to search out more information on these topics. I already had e-books and some information about these topics, but I had this feeling in my gut that I really needed to get as much information as possible.

Through the kind of keywords I typed in Google, many unscrupulous Internet marketers were able to smell blood! The kind of keywords I typed sent out a signal picked up by their keyword tools that I was desperate.

So, I would type in keywords like "how to make money quickly", "how to create a product today", "how to get traffic fast" etc, and these keywords at the time pulled up some sites selling the perfect solution for me.

I would enter an e-mail read a long sales letter and at the end I would be thrilled and excited because all that the letter promised could be obtained for a mere 97 USD.

So, I would click on the buy button to buy the e-book or course on traffic. The moment I would do that, I would immediately be taken to another website that said something like "Wait….you still need this extra tool…" So, I would buy this extra tool (297 USD) as well, and just when I thought it was all over, I had another message pop up saying that there was yet another indispensable tool needed to make the former two really work (997 USD), and then right when I would start wondering what other tool I was missing, another offer again was made that literally promised an all-done-for-you solution where all you had to do was buy this option, and you could forget about all the hard work and hassle of setting everything up for yourself.

So, basically, I had not received all the information up front. I had bought all these products, which I had to find time to read and apply. I had this horrible feeling of having been duped, but without the proof. I would then start blaming myself that I was probably not smart enough or that everybody else could succeed except me.

When I would go back to check my e-mails there would be yet another indispensable, one time offer that kept on proposing more products, tools and solutions to buy. I used to be furious with myself and with all these Internet Marketers who I felt did nothing but fleece their customers only to flaunt their wealth in front of everyone.

That's when I realized that the problem was bigger than that. The problem was systemic. It started with the constant offer from McDonalds to supersize, to add this and that etc. I realized that all these up sells were not new, they were part of both offline and online marketing strategies. But it was still up sell hell for me – I felt the heat and the pain every time.

And since I hate that feeling of deceiving or conning someone every time I tried to implement the systems that they taught to cash in on your customers failed woefully because I was doing this without conviction.

I was in conflict with myself, because it felt like I was just setting up mouse traps with stale cheese. So, that's when I started looking for more ethical ways to create and market my product and opportunities online.

In the process of chasing after the next new thing, I learnt ALOT of things, and everything in this book is the result of endless hours and tens of thousands of dollars spent on courses, e-books, trainings and the like. At the end of the day, it is not all that glitters that's gold. Whatever the product or service you are offering make sure the content is just as impressive as the packaging.

Think of packaging like the best Christmas wrapping paper. Most people do not remember the color or the texture of the wrapping paper that concealed their gift, but they remembered their gift though.

Understanding the Ethical Fundamentals of Marketing on the Internet

One of my first mentors who is now of late was a man called Corey Rudl. This guy was a genius when it came to Internet marketing. There were few guys out there who knew what they were talking about like he did. I still own and treasure his courses and videos.

One of the things Corey used to say was that people go to the Internet primarily to look for information, or find a solution to a problem or a need.

Can you offer a solution to a popular problem, but maybe using a creative format or delivery method, that will make you stand out from your competition?

What about the nature of your solution? If you are solving a big problem, then don't be afraid to spend time developing the quality of the product and the various formats in which you could put them (audio, video, workbooks, seminars etc).

If you don't care for e-books, then create audio products. Interview experts, have others interview you on the subject matter. Make training videos with Camtasia studio (a screen and voice recording software), make real training videos (you speaking in front of a camera). Just get creative in your delivery methods, and this will make you stand out from the crowd. It will be your USP (Unique Selling Point).

So, in creating your product you need to consider that the people who are coming online are looking for a solution to a problem. The more research you do (especially in forums and blog comments), the more you will be able to zero in on a specific problem, and this is what will give you the edge over your competitors. Your profile of your ideal customer should be very clear in your mind.

For example being a doctor is a general title, but being an ophthalmologist is even more specific. It means even though you have done the general training as a medical doctor, you are now specialized in eye care.

So, if you were to address the problems of ophthalmologist, you would not speak as if you were talking to all doctors. You would probably get an echo, but it will not be targeted enough.

In other words, you need to understand that a market is a group of clients/customers that have similar wants and desires, and that makes them the ideal target for certain kind promotional offers, and the market place is the place where you can have direct access to them.

There is no such thing as being too targeted. You need to be constantly looking for loopholes in a given niche or market. Do not conclude that a market is saturated just because the main need is being met. You should think about the need within the need.

For example, let's look at the car tuning industry. These guys capitalized on the need for personalization for car owners. The automotive industry was producing very nice cars, but which were too generic for many, so there was a need for additional personalization, and this is where the tuning experts came in.

Within the tuning industry you have even more subcategories. You have customization services for the external part of the car (Paint, rims, exhaust pipes, windows etc), and then you have customization for the internal part of the car (sound system, seats, engine etc). I am sure if you look into it you will find even more examples, either within this field or in other examples.

When you look online to identify your target market look with these lenses and apply these criteria. Offer these things to your prospects, and you will be amazed at how the market will respond to your products and services. The more targeted your products and services are the more conversion they will get.

Who is Your Ideal Prospect/Client and Where do You Find Them?

Ezines, Adswaps, Solo ads before even positioning yourself to sell a product or service, you need to clearly identify who your ideal customer is. That is why we talk about having targeted leads or prospects.

No matter what product you sell, you are going to need visitors, and not just any kind of visitors, but extremely targeted visitors.

There are tons of offers out there promising to send you hundreds of hits to your website for some low and ridiculous prices. The first time I saw these offers, I said to myself, well that could really help in jumpstarting my business.

It is only later that I discovered that this was untargeted traffic and that they were a bunch of "freeloaders". Needless to say that these advertisers never received another dime from me. I believe these offers continue to exist, because there continues to be newcomers to the market who do not know any better, and so I believe some of these companies continue to thrive on the ignorance of the masses.

In order to really sell properly to your ideal customer you need to go and find out where they hang out. You will find them in Forums, blog comments, eBay feedbacks, Amazon feedbacks, Face book pages and any other interactive social platform. By reading their comments, questions and feedbacks you will get a pretty clear idea of who your ideal customer is.

As a matter of fact, here are a few questions you can use as a frame to sort of visualize who your ideal customer is like so that you can really speak to them in a unique way:

1. What is their current occupation, what is their income bracket? Do they have any savings?

2. What do they like doing in their spare time….their hobbies, sports or recreational activities

3. What do they look like? Are they image conscious or not?

4. What is their outlook on their career, where do they see themselves 5 years from now, do they love or hate their job

5. Are they mostly women or men? Are they stay home mom's or professionals with very hectic schedules. Does is it even matter if they are male or female?

6. What are their dreams? What kind of things would they like to accomplish in life. Are they people of faith or not? What is it that they really love doing?

7. What is their level their technology IQ? In other words how comfortable are they with the computer and the Internet in general

8. When they buy things from the Internet, do they prefer digital versions or do they like receiving physical products

9. How motivated are they to do whatever it is you are offering?

10. Are they married and do they have support from their spouses in what they do?

11. Etc...etc...etc... you can add your own questions here.

Your ideal client has a favorite hangout spot on the Internet, and you need to be creative to find out where to find them. They hang out on their favorite blogs, on their favorite Face book pages and on their preferred forums.

They may or may not leave comments, but a post from you can bring them out through responses or views, and that will give you an idea of the interest in your subject matter while leaving an actual trace for them to get back to you.

Your ideal client is most likely part of an RSS Feed or a newsletter. The fastest way of getting maximum exposure is to put your message directly in front of what they already read without having them change their habits. It is just a way of providing them with another alternative to what they are already used to doing.

It's like walking down a boulevard of restaurants. It's like going to the food court of a shopping mall. People who go there go to eat, so you have a better chance of actually selling something to someone because you are well positioned.

That's what makes powerhouses like Ebay and Amazon so indomitable. Their customers are people who already have their credit cards in hand ready to buy. They come to these sites with the intention of buying something.

So, if you have a physical product that you want to sell, it absolutely makes sense to put this product right in front of them so that they may have yet another alternative to choose from.

Writing helpful articles, placing your ads in newspapers, in Ezines (newsletters), ad spaces, and other similar areas puts your message in front of your targeted audience, that's how you find your client and propose your product and service.

The bottom line is this, if you can learn as much as you can about your client, and sincerely invest yourself in finding solutions to their problems, fears and needs, then you would have done the hardest part. Plus, it is an ongoing exercise, people change and so do their needs, and desires, and the more you listen the more you will know how to adjust and provide appropriate responses and answers.

Why You Absolutely Need to Create Your Very Own Product or Service

People want to and love to work with experts. Someone who knows more than they do. It makes them feel secure, and it is extremely gratifying for them. One can almost compare the notion of working with an expert to the placebo effect.

The placebo effect is a term that is used in the medical field to describe the measurable health improvement of a patient after the intervention of "supposed" medical substance or procedure.

For example, if a patient is relieved from severe pain in the stomach after having taken a "powerful medical pill" supposed to eliminate the pain, then we call the patients healing a placebo effect. Why? Because the "powerful medical pill" was nothing more than crystallized starch.

I have actually experienced this placebo effect myself a few times.

One of these instances occurred in Jamestown, North Dakota. I was a Computer Science student at Jamestown College, and it had not been long since I had arrived in the States from Switzerland.

I was starting to fully integrate the culture, and among the things I think I fully integrated was the fast food industry! Among my favorites was Dominoes pizza.

Dominoes Pizza did exist in Switzerland, but it was really expensive. It was about 15-20 USD depending on the toppings you included, so it was not really the first choice.

So, when I arrived in Jamestown and realized that I could order Dominoes for 6.99 USD with all kinds of toppings, and that I even had the opportunity of having my Pizza free if they exceeded the 30 minute guarantee, I went nuts!

I think I must have ordered Dominoes Pizza every single evening for 3 consecutive months!

In the fourth month I woke up one morning with a terrible gut wrenching pain in my stomach – I was literally crying. I managed to crawl out of my bed and knock on one of my dorm mates door who immediately rushed me to the ER at the nearby hospital.

The pain kept increasing as we went to the hospital, but when we arrived at the hospital I was immediately put on a bed and had a whole bunch of nurses dressed in white bustling and hustling around me, telling me that everything was going to be just fine.

I can't explain how it happened, but the pain immediately disappeared. I could have walked off and gone right back to the college campus, but I had to undergo some tests and wait for the doctor to come.

When the doctor arrived, he could not find anything wrong with me no matter the testing techniques he used with his hand on my stomach.

That's when it dawned on me that the whole hospital environment, knowing that I would be dealing with people who already knew what they were talking about, was what brought a created an amazing peace of mind, which must have eventually trickled down to my stomach.

I can't explain this scientifically of course, but I remember that seeing all these white blouses all around me had made me feel extremely safe and reassured that I was not going to die.

So, working with an expert creates something in the mind of the non-expert that, not only makes them feel good or secure, but that can even propel them to competence. That is the key in succeeding in your online business, or in any business for that matter.

So it is in the Internet business world. Everybody is looking for somebody they can trust. Every client is going to be looking for these three things in you: **Credibility**, **trust** and **empathy**.

Remember the old sales adage we talked about that basically says that people tend to buy from people they know (Credibility), like (empathy) and Trust.

Building Credibility, Trust and Authority on the Internet
There is a TV Sprite commercial that says *"Obey your thirst....thirst is everything"*

Well, when it comes to having an online business, I would model the above mentioned quotation, but would say something like:

"Obey your image.....image is everything"

In other words, your image, your reputation on the Internet is what will make or break you.

How To Think And Become A Successful Webpreneur

Because of the impersonal nature of the Internet and the amount of scams that have emerged over the years from this medium, people are even more skeptical of any good thing coming from the Internet.

It's not that they don't believe, it's just that their « scam detector » or « scam radar » is on high alert. So the least wrong move will be swiftly punished and destroyed by online reputation assassins.

In no time your name and service will be smeared all over the Internet, and we all know how difficult it is to retrieve a good name or restore the reputation of someone who has been accused (be it falsely or not).

That is where the importance of ethical values such as integrity, honesty, service, humility, empowerment come into play. The truth of the matter is that no matter what you offer, whether it be the best thing since sliced bread and butter, you will always have critics. This is a given!

When you have put in your heart, soul and spirit into a product or service that you now want to make available to the public, be ready for disgruntled and dissatisfied customers, this is just part of the trade. Even the greatest entrepreneurs with the greatest products face these issues. With the advent of the Iphone, IPAD and IMAC, Steve Jobs knew that he wanted to revolutionize the industry while making a profit.

 Even though Steve Jobs had a very strong following, there were still quite a few people out there who were not only unhappy with the closed nature of the apple products, but who literally hated his guts for that and other things.

So, since you know you are going to be criticized anyway, you might as well focus on those that will really love your product, and try not to please everyone because you will be unable to.

Bill Gates tried to market to the masses, and it worked for a little while just like any new craze, but eventually what works best is targeted marketing, and this is why Steve Jobs stuck to his guns until his products became main stream.

So building authority and credibility on the Internet starts off with people getting to know you very well. They need to know that you have nothing but their best interest at heart. They need to know that you are like them, and that you understand them.

This is what we see in politics....the politicians that win elections are those that have mastered the art of relating to their voters. They know how to speak their language and they know their frustrations and their pain. The moment a politician understands this, he has already crushed his competition!

What and who you are speaks a million times louder than what you say. Master this and you will master the art of authentic selling.

You will have droves of like minded customers lining up to « interact » with you. Sell yourself ethically and authentically and you will sell all the products you want, to as many customers as you want.

You need to ask yourself the question whether or not you would buy anything from yourself. Why should people buy anything from you. What makes you different from the millions of people online who are pretty much offering the same thing or something similar? What makes you different?

Remember that people buy from people they know like and trust. What makes one sales man in a best buy store sell more electronic appliances than the other? Probably because he knows how to listen, present well and really relate to the customer....

Think about the last time you bought something with the help of a sales agent. Was he helpful? What did you like the most about the guy or girl? Those are the things you need to focus on and amplify in the way you will now present yourself.

What's in it for your customer? What is the added value they receive by dealing with you?

How To Think And Become A Successful Webpreneur

Here is the thing. If you really want to stand out from the crowd then you are going to need to crawl out of your anonymous closet, and put a face, an avatar or a powerful logo or some kind of visual representation out there for people to identify to you.

You will then have to make your personality stand out a little bit more by having your very own style and personal touch. Yes...you will need to get a little personal with your clients or prospects.

Don't forget that you are online to sell some kind of service or product – so, yes....you are in sales. However, you need to redefine what being a salesman/saleswoman means for you.

When you really look deep down into the deontology of sales, you will realize that being in sales doesn't mean you have to pretend, lie and be slimy. No, you really just only need to be an excellent listener, and extremely relational. By mastering these aspects of your people skills, you will have customers lining up to buy ONLY from you.

Your personal brand (your blog, your Face book page, your twitter page, your YouTube page, your LinkedIn page etc) is your check book. So, you need to make sure that you express your personality and your true self in whatever it is that you will be offering online. People will first buy you before they buy your product.

Secondly, if you really want to be able to offer the best value to your customers, then you are going to need to invest in yourself though education, training and mindset....all of which is included right here in this book.

Let's say you go out to buy a cell phone and you don't know which model to choose from. The sales agent who will approach you and who will ask you the right questions and really listen to what you want to use the phone for will probably be the one that gets your purchase. Why? because this person not only knows the specifications of the phones in his aisle, but he also knows exactly which of these phones will best match the requirements you have given him. These same principles that you see operating in the offline world are definitely applicable in your online business.

Here are a few examples of personal branding:

http://www.jamieoliver.com/ - Jamie is in the cooking and recipe niche – it's his passion!

http://chrisguillebeau.com/ - Chris dislikes the mass mentality syndrome and is challenging the status quo of rules

http://www.redheadwriting.com/ - Erika just loves to rant, and her rants ring a bell with millions of others

http://www.lewishowes.com/ - Lewis is the LinkedIn Go-to-guy. He is the example of mastering one thing and becoming an expert at that thing

http://lebronjames.com/ - If you follow baskteball, then "the king" needs no introduction

http://www.lindabrodskymd.com/ - Linda is a pediatric surgeon who understands that she can harness the power of the Internet to attract thousands of clients either to her offices or to her book.

http://garyvaynerchuk.com/ - Gary is a social media and wine expert! Interesting combination. Living out your passion and becoming wealthy through it is Gary's expertise – A true powerhouse in the domain !

http://www.problogger.net/ - Darren Rose if one of the few to burst out cause a stir on the blogging scene in regards to the earning potential of blogging

http://mostlylisa.com/ - Lisa is all about showcasing her work because she is passionate about images, photoshop and the like, her passion is contagious.

http://nerdfitness.com/blog/ - Steve's angle is pretty unique. He knows there are fitness sites out there for all the buffs and popular guys out there, but what about all the nerds who would also like a hero and some tips for themselves? That's where Steve comes in. It is truly his unique selling point (USP)

How To Think And Become A Successful Webpreneur

http://www.richardessi.com - (Yep...that's me!) Richard is all about empowering newbie online entrepreneurs who want to have a profitable presence online, and who want to do this ethically. Richard loves to empower others. His passion is motivating and encouraging others to express their true self and challenge the status quo.

So, what's the bottom line of building credibility and authority in your online business? Well, you are going to have to invest in yourself, so that you do actually have some added value to bring to the table.

Next, you are going to need stand out from the crowd by sharing on a subject that you are passionate about, thereby establishing your very own unique selling point (USP) which will make you even more original. Don't try to follow the crowd. Don't be a crowd pleaser.

Stay away from mass psychology. Mass psychology is more subtle and powerful than you think. It is that mentality that makes everybody want to do the same thing, react the same way.

So, just because everyone seems to be doing it doesn't make it good or effective. Know your "why" behind every action, so that no matter what you have to face in terms of challenge or difficulty, you will not back down because you know exactly WHY you are doing what you are doing.

Knowing your why creates a strong conviction in what it is you do, and without conviction you will eventually wear yourself out. Do not do things by obligation, do the hard work of finding out what your deepest convictions are, and operate within those parameters. If you do this, you will become a force to reckon with – an unstoppable force.

The Targeted Traffic and List Building Secrets of the Multi Millionaires

The most recurrent question I have seen in the online business arena is "HOW DO I GET TRAFFIC?"

Well, let me answer that question in the simplest way possible. There are 3 general ways to get traffic to your website, and they are the following:

Paid Traffic

This is the kind of traffic that will cost you, but will also be quite effective. It is in fact one of the fastest ways to get traffic. This is in the form of Pay Per Click (PPC) through the Google Adwords program or through the Yahoo Paid search program, and other search engine related paid traffic.

There is also other paid solutions like placing ads in newsletters (Ezines), or classified ads sites, placing banner ads in the same locations and a sleuth of other paid ad alternatives.

Self-Generated Traffic

This is the kind of traffic that depends on the effort you put in. It has to do with Search Engine Optimization (SEO) which is basically the art of writing so that it is search engine friendly. In other words, you write your content on your website or in articles or press releases in such a way that the Google spiders will crawl and pick up your content and make them available to the searchers.

You also have the social media techniques, which involve using sites like Face book, Twitter, YouTube and LinkedIn to generate extremely targeted leads to your offer.

Joint Ventures

This is where you borrow traffic by finding common grounds and creating win-win situations with other like minded entrepreneurs. This is actually a business to business move. You have to find out what your potential partner wants or is lacking, and fill that need. If for example, you have a product, you might want to offer your product at a 100% commission rate so that your partner keeps all the profits, as long as he advertises your product to his list. You might think this unfair in the beginning, but you would have invested in your future success. The truth is that if your product is really good, then the people who bought it and used it will now know like and trust you. By this time, you would have built a list with all those who bought your product even though all the profits went to your joint venture partner.

All you will have to do is create a new product. Once this new product is created, the only thing you will need to do is send an e-mail to your database of newly acquired and satisfied customers, who will now gladly come to your website and buy your product, and this time you can choose to keep all the products, or you could yet again find some additional joint venture partners and offer them 30-50 percent profit if they can promote your product to their list.

Believe it or not, many Internet millionaires have been created by using each of the above mentioned techniques.

Now, every professional Internet Entrepreneur will tell you how important a list is.

Many people worry about getting ongoing traffic to their website. While it is a legitimate concern, it is not the most important thing.

Getting traffic to your website is not the most complicated, the real catch is converting these visitors into faithful and loyal customers.

The real objective behind your traffic is that you want them loving what you have to offer, and have them coming back for more. What's the point of having thousands of different visitors coming to your site daily, and not even spending more than 30 seconds on your site only to leave the same rate as they came in without them having bought anything or leaving their contact details for further follow up.

There is a free tool that Google offers to every website owner that is called Google analytics. This script is a traffic analyzer tool that analyzes your traffic. Basically, it gives you vital information on what brought your visitors to your site, how long they spent on your site, what peaked their interest the most, and so much more.

So, let's say you have a site on growing roses. The Google analytics tool will help you identify what search phrase actually brought them to your site. This search phrase is what is commonly known in Internet Marketing circles as **keywords**.

Keywords are your best friends. Keywords are what tell you what exactly your customer is looking for. The nature of the keyword can literally tell you if they are just browsing for information of if they are actually ready to buy.

For example a person just browsing the Internet for DSLR cameras will type in a general search phrase related to the camera. So, by typing in "Canon DSLRs" the customer may just want some info on the various models of the Canon DSLR cameras.

I am not saying that a person typing in this search phrase could not be a potential buyer. He may be, but even if he is a potential buyer, he is not yet in the "buying phase" of the sales cycle.

The "buying phase" of the sales cycle is when the client has probably read all the reviews and is pretty much ready to buy. His search phrase will be more like "Canon 7d vs Canon 60d" or "Cheap Canon 7d" or even better

How To Think And Become A Successful Webpreneur

"Canon 7d wholesale" or yet again "Canon 7d + best price". I am sure you get the idea.

So now that you have your keywords, you know exactly what phrases to use in your blog posts, your articles and all written content that you will ever publish online. Now, you will speaking directly to your prospects at the exact moment you need them to act.

In order to really grasp the power of building a list, you need to expand your profit horizon and see the big picture. An immediate sale to your visitor great, but it could be better.

Marketing statistics in general, be they online or offline, state that a person needs to see a message 6-7 times before really buying into the message. That is why companies invest millions in commercials because they know that your subconscious mind will eventually integrate their message as something familiar, and when they will be exposed to multiple choices, their product will stand out because your mind will recognize their product as being something familiar.

So, how do you get your message repeatedly in front of your customers right in their living rooms or bedrooms like the "big boys" do? Well, that's where e-mail marketing kicks in. E-mail marketing is the avenue that opens up to you once you have built a list.

Your objective is to have every visitor to your site leave their name and e-mail address so that you have a way of getting back to them and building a relationship with them. If you have noticed already, you will see that the majority of websites have what you call an opt-in box.

This is a small box or a field that asks you to leave your name and e-mail address to receive additional information or in some cases, you have access to a FREE gift for leaving your e-mail address.

Their objective is simply to continue to build a relationship with you so that you can get to know, like and trust them. Unfortunately, many of these companies or individuals while they never sell your information, will bombard you with more promotional products than you can handle. It's a pity because the readers on the other end feel a little abused and disgusted by the overbearing selling pitches of every e-mail.

You need to distance yourself from what I consider overly aggressive and unethical practices, and build long lasting relationships with your customers by providing them with valuable and actionable content, not just endless e-mails of sales pitches!

If you want to see an amazing and creative use of list building techniques on one website check out Martin Lewis's site: http://www.moneysavingexpert.com/

If you look closely at his site you will realize that every single page has an e-mail optin box which is directly related to the particular subject matter. This way, the person putting in their e-mail address knows exactly what information they will be receiving, and will actually be looking forward to receiving this information rather than saying "not again…." or "now what??"

Another form of list building is through using what is commonly known as landing pages. I am sure you have bumped into one of these before. For example, check out Groupon's landing page : http://www.groupon.com/subscriptions/new?division_p=st-johns

They collect your zip code and then your e-mail address, this way they know they will always be able to send you their latest offers, and keep you informed of the latest developments, and you will give them this information willingly, because it will be of great use to you.

No matter the nature of your sales funnel, the collecting of e-mail addresses is one the most important things you will have to do in your online business, so you really need to take this seriously.

In fact, if you approach certain list owners (you can find them in Ezine directories or forums), you will be able to rent their lists to market your product, service or landing page, so that you in turn can build your list, so there is no excuse to not get started with this technique.

So, even if you don't have a completed product just yet, you can send a compelling message to a rented list (an ad space you bought in a newsletter) about the information which is to come and have people signing up on your landing page, and receiving helpful and valuable content from your auto responder.

So, let me recap. List building is one of the most important skill you will need to learn in your online business. It is the art of finding customers, converting them and making them faithful to your product and services.

Quite simply, here is what you will need to do to set up your list building campaign:

Landing Pages

Landing pages are simply one page websites whose only objective is to collect names and e-mail addresses and in some cases telephone numbers.

You have probably seen one of these if you have been looking at different ways to make money online. In some cases, it is just a video explaining a concept, an Idea or a product, and for more information you are requested to enter your name and e-mail address. Once you enter your details, you are usually taken over to the next page to claim your gift or to obtain additional information on what was been presented on the entry page.

Once you enter your e-mail address your e-mail is automatically recorded in what is commonly known as an auto responder. An auto responder is a personalized e-mail management database system that you rent that collects the names and e-mail addresses that you send to it.

The reason it is called an auto responder is because it will automatically send the messages that you would have inputted prior to this in the system. So, you would have basically pre-programmed 5-100+ messages in your auto responder that are programmed to be sent out to those e-mail addresses daily, weekly or monthly, all depending on your preferences. Ideally, it is good to have an e-mail go out at least once a week.

This eliminates the need to sit down and write a personal e-mail to each and every one of your prospects as they sign up, especially since many of them will be signing up while you are sleeping or away from your computer. It's like having your own personal secretary that does all the administrative work for you, while you focus on growing your business.

You can of course choose to send out some improvised messages from time to time, but the popularity and efficiency of auto responders is being able to send out e-mails automatically to new subscribers.

Of course the subscribers cannot reply to the auto responder, but it is always great to include an option in your e-mail for your subscribers to reply or comment if they so choose, this allows you to really stay in touch with your customer base, and maintains a high level of interactivity which is crucial to your growth and success.

You cannot envisage building a list without an auto responder. I have tried a whole bunch of auto responders in the past, and you are free to choose which one you prefer. The main auto responders I have dealt with are Aweber, Getresponse, Icontact, and 1shoppingcart. There are several others, but these are the ones I have personally dealt with either as the sender or the receiver.

Today, I personally use Getresponse.

Make your list building campaign as simple as possible. From the optin/squeeze/landing page, make things clear and simple for your prospects. They should know exactly what to do on that page which is to enter their name and e-mail address. Then when they receive an e-mail message from you, it should be filled with valuable content that is linked to the reason they entered their e-mail address in the first place.

Keep things very straight to the point and simple. Google's search engine format is an amazing example of how to keep things really simple. All you have is a rectangular box to enter your search terms for whatever it is you want, there are no distractions, at least not until you have entered your search term. I think this concept can be mirrored on your squeeze/optin/landing page.

There are tons of books and products on list building, and they can be very detailed and technical.

However, what I want you to do is take action. Don't be afraid to make mistakes. In fact mistakes can be one heck of a teacher. It's part of what will count as your experience and expertise.

Remember, that you are investing in yourself so that you can give value to your customers. Part of the value you can give can come from the mistakes you have made. So, don't be scared to take action even if you feel you don't have ALL the details, at least get the basics and learn as you go.

If you buy all the books on list building and try to understand the science, the psychology and all the different techniques that exist out there, you will learn quite a bit, but you will realize that more information calls for even more information, and at the end you will end up suffering from information overload just in that area, and you will equally suffer from paralysis of analysis, which simply means you have so much information in your head that you no longer know what to do with it....and trust me I am speaking from experience.

All you need to know about list building for now is that it is a way for you build a relationship with your customer base. Spend your time focusing on the messages you want to preprogram in your auto responder. If you want you can look at the newsletters you are subscribed to and get ideas from there, but above all, be YOURSELF, and in the messages you send make sure your personality transpires. People are drawn more to who you are than what you actually say!

10 THE POWER OF AUTHENTIC RELATIONAL MARKETING

Authenticity is <u>Very</u> Good – Be Obsessed With Building Real and Authentic Relationships with Your Clients

Theodore Roosevelt once said:

"Nobody cares how much you know, until they know how much you care"

As for Maya Angelou, she is known to have said:

"If you find it in your heart to care for somebody else, you would have succeeded"

This is where the majority of online business entrepreneurs get it wrong! This is where they shoot themselves in the foot!

The product, the service the information they provide right from the beginning is never to empower or to really help the customer, but instead make the customer dependent on them for solutions, so they can make as much money as they can on this customer.

How To Think And Become A Successful Webpreneur

Some people may consider this clever marketing, but I don't. I believe the customer should always be clearly informed on the intentions of the seller at all times, so that they always feel and know that the seller has their best interest at heart.

Failure to show the customer how much you truly care is a simple recipe for losing credibility and authority, and without these two, your ethical success online is doomed to fail.

Many newbie entrepreneurs fail to see the big and long term picture. They fail to understand that it is not so much how much you start, but it is more about how you finish. It is more about projecting yourself 3-10 years down the road. If you are an entrepreneur, be it online or offline, and you devise your strategies and build like this, your success becomes inevitable, because in doing so, you have just killed the "microwave" mentality that shapes the actions and decisions of 90% of Online Entrepreneurs.

Most Internet Entrepreneurs think that because they are on the Internet everything is going to be so much simpler and so much faster, and so most tend to underestimate the time it will take them to achieve the results they need, and in doing so, they raise their expectations to unrealistic levels, and at the same time make themselves vulnerable to all kinds of pie-in-the-sky theories and get rich quick schemes.

As I mentioned earlier, if you are going to be making any kind of money online, you are going to have to understand that you will be buying and selling something, or you will be paid for having matched up a buyer and a seller. Either way, money is made when there is an exchange of money for a good or service. This is clearly understood in the offline business world, and the same principle applies on the Internet.

So, if you are going to be selling and facilitating the sales of goods and services then it means you will be dealing with REAL people. These people have REAL issues, and will be needing REAL solutions. Don't fall into the common lie that is propagated online that all you need is a list, and once you have that list they will spend their time and their life checking your every mail waiting to buy the next product that you will be peddling! Don't fall into that mentality that has spread all over the Internet business marketing world, where the common understanding is that the people on these lists that you will be building are nothing more than credit card numbers waiting to make you rich!

Again, I need to re-emphasize this point, because this is one of the backbones of every Internet business.

"The money is in the list."

As I mentioned earlier, if you have browsed a few Internet business forums, then you've probably heard that before.

While this remains a fact, the message communicated behind is not entirely true, and it can be very misleading.

The number one way to build an authentic and caring relationship with your customer base is to publish a newsletter, or something similar where they will be hearing from you, on the latest information that you may have that will be of interest **TO THEM**!

Notice I put "**TO THEM**" in bold, and this is on purpose!

The biggest obstacle you face and have to overcome when you publish a newsletter or put any free or paid information out there is the fact that people have gotten used to getting junk (from your competitors) disguised as helpful free or paid information.

Many writers put out sub standard information simply because they're writing from a mentality of "I gotta get paid" and when you do that, you completely forget about the people you're writing to and start to concentrate on you and what you want.

That's a surefire recipe for disaster.

"Whenever you write anything for your subscribers, website visitors and customers don't write with the sole intention of getting a check.

How To Think And Become A Successful Webpreneur

Getting checks is nice but your business lives <u>or</u> dies based on how many people <u>believe</u> you genuinely want to help them achieve their goals."

Without an effort from *you* to show your readers **that you value them enough to part with real information** and that you see them as more than just a dollar sign, you're going to be lumped in a group with all the rest of your competitors with a big sign on your forehead marked "Will Do Anything For Commissions".

What you need from your list is a relationship. And in every working relationship, there is a mutual exchange, maybe more from one of the parties, but there is an exchange. It is not a one-way lane. This is how you build a dynamic and interactive following of people who know how much you care, and will therefore want to obtain as much information and help from you as possible.

So, these type of **Responsive** readers are born from conscious efforts to build a solid relationship with them. People connect with other people. Not mindless robots that only want commission checks.

Now don't get me wrong.

I'd love for you to buy the products I recommend, but I'm not going to force that on you. When I do enough of the right things in your eyes, **I will have <u>earned</u> the right** to ask you for your money in the form of commission checks from other products and services that I think could be helpful to you.

The big thing is that I have to earn that right by giving up good information that is of actual use to you. When you write anything you expect other people to read, the same thing applies to you.

If you're going to create information full of affiliate links then you're completely missing the point of what it takes to get people to value what you have to say.

I've done that in the past and it is **nowhere near as effective** as what I'm about to show you. If you want people to eagerly anticipate your next email with every intention of jumping on any products or services you recommend, you should follow the three rules I'm about to lay down for you because that's entirely possible to accomplish.

All the chapters in this book are important, but this particular chapter is one of the most if not the most important chapter when it comes down to the mentality you must adopt when dealing with customers.

I have nothing against giving you specific techniques and strategies because **they are important** but they are **never** more important than the thought process that went into creating them.

Throughout this exhaustive and final chapter I'll do my best to give you the overall thought process I have when I sit down to write. By doing that, you will be able to learn how to come up with your own specific ideas based on the concepts I'll show you.

What you will discover are proven concepts (i.e concepts that never stop working) based on the nature of the people you sell to. People can change a lot of things about themselves but their nature isn't usually one of them. People can go against their nature (for short periods of time) but rarely can they change it.

In the future you should make a conscious effort to try and **understand why** something is done instead of just copying what you see someone else successfully doing. There's always something more beneath the surface that you can study and learn from.

Let's look at three practical ways to establish a genuine and authentic relationship with your reader base or subscribers:

Relationship Marketing Principle #1: No Matter What You Are Selling Or Giving, Do Your Best To Make Your Intentions Crystal Clear From The Start

When people sign up to your newsletter, the first letter they get should be a personal message from **you** to **them** telling them **what they can expect** as a subscriber and **why** it's a good idea to stay subscribed and read every single email you send them.

Believe me, almost no one does this!

Your first message sets the tone for **everything** you do later. If you don't set the right tone up front, it's going to take you a lot longer to "warm up" your readers before they'll buy something from you.

When you make your first few emails about **them** and **their needs**, they'll start to wonder if you have something for them to buy. That's a good position to be in because it puts your readers in a more receptive mood when you actually do present them with a direct offer.

Put your own agenda on hold for a minute.

Forget about your interest, and really engage with your readers and provide a real and practical solution to their problem and their need.

That's why I stress so much on the whole issue of your personal development, and your state of mind when offering your products and services. If you don't have a positive image about yourself, you will communicate that to your customers, and they will simply react to the image that you are projecting to them about yourself. How do you perceive yourself? In this particular instance your self- perception can and will be contagious.

Remember this... **Perception is reality**. In other words, whatever someone **believes** to be the truth is the truth to him or her.

With that in mind, isn't it in your best interest to "control" (as much as possible) what your readers believe to be the truth? You can control (to a great extent) how people perceive and react to you by carefully presenting yourself the way you want them to see you….

Won't it be so much easier, if you didn't have to pretend to be someone who cared, and instead be someone who REALLY cared?

If you want your readers to respond to you in a positive way, you have to give them a solid reason to by giving them what **they** want **before** expecting to get what **you** want. This will become a lot clearer as you read on. Remember what we said earlier…people care only when they realize that you truly care for them.

Here is a story of what happened to Edmund, a fellow Internet Entrepreneur friend of mine.

To a certain extent, many people will have a preconceived idea in their head of what Edmund is supposed to be like just by looking at him, but since he believes that the opinion he has of myself is the only relevant one, that's the one he tends to portray in the most favorable way.

Here is an incident he talks about…

One night (about 2:00 am) while he was on his way home from a friend's house he stopped to get some gas. Turns out, the gas station he went to wasn't accepting gas cards that night so he wanted to use the ATM inside.

Edmund walked up to the window, introduced himself to the attendant on duty and then asked the 5' 5" or so guy behind the counter if he could come in and use the ATM because his card wasn't working (pointing out to his car) and that he needed some cash to buy gas.

****

Side Note: Knowing that people generally tend to care about themselves and what they need before even thinking about you and what you need, he gave the guy what he wanted before expecting anything in return.

****

Even though the attendant needed Edmund's money for gas, what was more important to him was to know for a fact that Edmund would not be a physical threat to him. So Edmund purposely presented himself in a way that allowed the attendant to see him as someone who not only would not hurt him but as someone whom he could trust enough to let his guard down with.

Whether that was true or not, it was that person Edmund purposely presented for the attendant to see.

Nothing about Edmund's behavior or the look in his eyes betrayed the image he purposely put in front of the attendant. Everything he said and did was coherent with the idea Edmund wanted the attendant to have of him.

Edmund already had enough money to get some gas (more than enough to get home) but saw this as an opportunity to see if he could get into the locked gas station based on his attitude and his words.

If the attendant didn't let Edmund in he just would have gone to another station, the attendant would have lost a sale for the gas station and Edmund would have lost time by going to another station, all because Edmund did not make the effort to present himself properly.

Now think about this...

Edmund asked a guy smaller than himself who was protected by a locked door and bulletproof glass if he would let him (a man he didn't know) into the store around 2:00 in the morning.

Now, Edmund would have completely understood if the attendant didn't open the door but he did it anyway......and on his way in, the attendant said these two things:

1. "Well, I guess it's ok because you don't look like you're going to rob me."

My question to you is..... how did this attendant come to this conclusion ? What is it that Edmund said and did that completely reassured him?

Simple. **Edmund made his intentions clear to the attendant before asking for what he wanted.**

2. The second thing he said was to another guy behind Edmund that tried to walk into the store...

"Get back or I'll call the cops. You can't come in!"

Again, why would the attendant let **Edmund** in but not the other guy behind him? Edmund and the other guy were both 6'+ 200+ men trying to get into the store and Edmund was allowed inside the store while the other guy had to leave under the threat of calling the cops.

It's actually quite simple. The gas station attendant based his belief that Edmund wasn't going to rob him, simply on Ed's belief that he wasn't going to rob him.

Could Ed have been threatened as well? Of course, but Ed did what was necessary to get his true intentions across to the attendant.

What does any of that have to do with creating the type of relationship with your readers that allows you to get them to buy basically anything you choose to promote?

Think about this for a moment.....

People have nothing to base their opinions of you on other than the person/image you purposely **or <u>accidentally</u>** present for them to judge. As soon as you do the same things most of your competitors do, you get labeled as one of them even if you're not. That is why we talked about the power of being YOU. Don't be a copy cat ! Be yourself, and you will be unique and original.

That's why it's so important to make your intentions crystal clear right from the start. Do something that your competition hasn't thought of doing because they're only thinking of themselves and what <u>they</u> want. Not what their readers need from them **first**.

Believe it or not, people can pick up on your intentions.

If they can't (because you haven't made your intentions clearly known) they'll just guess at what your intentions are and for whatever reason, whenever someone has to guess at what your intentions are, they will almost **never** think of anything positive. Why is that ? Well, that's simply because the average human being living and breathing on this earth has been emotionally hurt quite a few times, and is therefore leery of anything that requires him/her to trust.

****

Side Note: Did you notice how many times I've used the word because so far? Some of that is natural conversation but a lot of it was purposely put there to (shut your brain off) get you to automatically accept what I said before it. I'm purposely leading the way and not giving your brain a chance to question me.

****

In other words, I was filling in the gaps between what I said and what I wanted you to hear so that you wouldn't consciously think about or guess about certain things. I told you **A** is true because of **B** instead of just saying A is true. If I had just said A is true then you would have tried to figure out on your own if it was but when I say A is true because of whatever, people generally accept whatever answer you give them even if it doesn't really make sense.

Whenever you leave gaps in what you say, people will try to connect the dots on their own. That's what the brain does. It fills in the gaps between what you say and what you don't say with the most logical (and most often the worst) explanation of what you mean.

Your intentions (or at least what you can get others to believe your intentions are) have the power to move them to do things for **you** they wouldn't dream of doing for anyone else.

To borrow from the earlier example, Ed made it clear to the attendant what his intentions were while the other guy wanting to get into the store **simply tried to walk in behind him.**

He just wanted to get into the store and he wasn't thinking about **the feeling of security the attendant needed**. That led the attendant to automatically **assume** that he was up to no good.

The only thing that separated Ed from the other guy was the fact that Ed introduced myself, carefully stated his intentions and asked the attendant if he would help him out and gave him a "because" reason.

This is applicable in every circumstance.

So you will need to ask yourself some honest questions.

Are you just trying to quietly slip into people's email inbox or are you introducing yourself and clearly stating your intentions for being there so they can feel comfortable about letting you into their space?

Unfortunately, people have been conditioned not to expect much from free information so clearly stating your intentions is an absolute must. If you don't, people will automatically assume that you only write to them so you can send them advertising.

If you writing to them just to be able to peddle your products and services, then you need to re-engineer your strategy to make sure that your true intentions transpire in how you write.

How To Think And Become A Successful Webpreneur

You will see all kinds of courses, training modules emphasizing on how you should **build your list** without necessarily teaching you what to do with your list as you build it.

Just about everyone who joins your list will at least read the first message you send to them and make up their minds about you based on that first email. Knowing this, doesn't it now seem obvious that **your first email is the most important** and that you should do everything in your power to make sure people have the right "picture" of you and your intentions in their heads so they don't draw their own conclusions about you?

Letting people draw their own conclusions is almost never good.

Don't leave it up to your readers to figure out why you have a newsletter because they won't come up with a good reason. **Tell them why.** Tell them **why** they should want to be a subscriber/stay subscribed and **why** they should listen to what you have to say.

Practice making that extra effort to positively influence the way you are "coming across". Practice is the only way you're going to learn how to do this. You will start to understand (just like I now do) that **you can make people see you <u>any</u> way you want them to**.

How else could Ed be escorted inside of a closed gas station by an attendant who told someone else directly behind him(who looked like Ed) to leave or the cops would be called out to arrest him?

The **only** major difference between me and the other guy who had to leave under the threat of arrest was the way that I came across to the attendant. I came across exactly like I purposely wanted to.

It was a **calculated effort** on Ed's part was to project himself as being someone who the person on duty could feel comfortable about coming out from behind the bulletproof glass and unlocking the door for.

If **Ed**, a regular guy could do that, what could <u>you</u> do if you made the effort to change how people perceive you?

And apparently that isn't the only time Ed has been escorted inside of a locked gas station late at night. He says he tried a few more times (just to prove the first time wasn't a fluke) and got let in four times again where the attendant quickly locked the door behind him. It didn't work every time, but it worked more times than it failed, and that was enough for him to draw a conclusion.

There are three things you can do right now to change the way people see you. How people see you mainly has to do with the type of person you **purposely** or **accidentally** present for them to see.

With that in mind …

1. Evaluate your current image. Are your readers doing what you want them to do? Are they buying from you? Are they at least taking the time to look at the products you recommend to them? If not, take an honest look at yourself and ask yourself if you're presenting a person that is <u>worth</u> (or appears to be worth) listening to and buying from.

If not, take steps to make yourself **be** that type of person. Use the next two steps I'm giving you to portray the image of someone who your readers can see themselves looking to for **answers**, **guidance** and **support** on the way to achieving their goals. All people really care about is their goals and **anyone who <u>seems</u>** to want to help them reach those goals.

People will evaluate you based on how much they think you can help or hurt them on the way to what <u>they</u> want. That's why it's so vitally important that you give the best information you can.

2. Take a good look at your surroundings. Generally you want to do the opposite of what the majority of other people do because being a part of the "herd" will get you what the "herd" gets. A small share of whatever they're fighting over. You have to remove yourself from the group and do what it takes to show your readers that **you are different** from the average free information publishing, commission-hungry, only care about themselves marketers out there.

Only people who do what others aren't doing get noticed. Period. If you're doing the same thing everyone else is doing then why would potential buyers pay any attention to you at all? You cannot have a "me too" business. Take some time to figure out what others in your market (your competitors) are doing so you can see how to consciously make yourself look better than they do.

It's as simple as that. What you want to do is put yourself in a position where your readers see that **you** are making an effort to connect with them while the majority of the other newsletters and email courses they're subscribed to are full of ads, recycled junk written by someone who's desperate for a commission check.

3. Figure out what your readers want and give it to them without thinking so much about what's in it for you. I know that doesn't sound right but what you have to understand is that people are loyal to other people who are loyal to them. You can't expect your readers to do something for you when you aren't willing to do something for them first so **you** have to be willing to be the one to initiate the relationship. Extend **your** hand and invite your readers to accept your invitation.

Your main job is to serve your readers. Not to get them to buy from you. They **will** buy, but only when they feel like you've done a good enough job of catering to their needs **first**.

Your "Why" Must be Bigger than You!

Are you really looking to build a loyal following that will be with you for the next 5-10 + years, or are you looking for a list of people to whom you can send out ads for whatever products you happen to be promoting at the moment?

You've been told that building a list with thousands of subscribers on it is the way to make money online. While partly true, the other part of the equation has to do with how many people on your list value your opinion enough to go out and buy something you're promoting.

So again, If I were to ask you... "Why do you publish free information?"

Your first answer should be:

"To **SERVE** the needs of the people who have taken the time to join my list."

They didn't have to join....

No one forced them to....

Only by taking an active interest in the needs of your readers will they in turn take an active interest in **your** needs. Sounds simple but it's easy to get blinded by the dollar sign and forget that actual people are subscribed to your list. Not mindless robots with checks and credit cards in hand, salivating to buy your products or services.

When you can figure out what the needs of your readers are and strive to fill those needs, you won't have any problems making as much money as you want with your list.

Relationship Marketing Principle #2: Make Your Subscribers Feel Like They Can Talk To You And That You Actually Care About What They Have To Say

One of the easiest to implement yet most overlooked ways to get people to warm up to you and feel like you value them and want to help them is to ask them simple questions. Everybody's favorite subject is himself or herself so why not show some interest?

Ask questions and do things that require some sort of interaction from your readers. It doesn't really matter what you ask. You can ask questions that are completely unrelated to what your newsletter is about so long as you get people to respond.

When you **get them used to doing things you ask them to do**, no matter what it is, it's easy for them to keep doing things you ask them to do like buy the products you recommend.

The more you can get your readers to communicate with you, the more they will feel like they know and can trust you.

A relationship (as far as an online newsletter or email course goes) is nothing more than two people (you and each individual subscriber) knowing what their place is in relation to each other.

You are the provider of helpful information and someone who wants to help your reader succeed at something. You must get that across.

Your reader is someone who will learn to trust your advice and listen to your recommendations because you have built up a history of doing things that **seem** to benefit them more than they **seem** to benefit you. That doesn't necessarily have to be true, as long as it **seems** like it's the truth to your readers.

Remember, perception (or what people believe) is the only truth that really matters as far as they're concerned.

The Internet is a cold and distant place.

That's actually to your advantage because if you can consistently get across to your readers that you are a **real** person with **real** concerns (just like them) and you know what it's like for them to be in the situation they're in because you've been there, you won't have any trouble getting people to warm up to you.

People in general tend to like others who look out for them because people (again, in general) think about themselves first. If it **seems** like another person is looking out for them first then that person will automatically take a high position in their eyes.

In other words, when you're writing, not every link in it has to be an affiliate link for a product you'll get paid from.

Understand this...

Your readers are buying products and services **all the time** that aren't putting money in your pockets **so it doesn't hurt you at all** to tell them about a product or service that you won't make money from.

This sets you up **to make money** when you do have something to recommend that **will** put a commission check in your pockets.

To set yourself up to make money you have to give, give, give and then give some more. Now it's important to note that I'm not saying that you have to give everything away.

Giving (as I'm using the term) means to give of yourself. Share stories with your readers, point them to helpful resources and let them know about things they probably haven't found on their own.

In other words, offer your guidance. That's what they signed up to your mailing list for. Not for a bunch of ads they can find on their own.

There's no point in building a list if your readers don't think you care about them. You should. Otherwise you don't deserve to have them as subscribers. When you give to your list, you **always** get back much more in return so you're actually being selfish by being unselfish. Knowing that you will get back more than you give ahead of time allows you to focus on giving.

There are some publishers I listen to above all others and when I took the time to try and figure out why, it hit me. They all do one thing that now seems so obvious.

Something **you** may feel compelled NOT to do. They all give me valuable information many times without promoting any products in some of the emails they send me.

They give me pages and pages of content I can actually do something with. When they do have an affiliate link in an email I don't even care they'll be getting a commission from my purchase because of all the great content surrounding that affiliate link.

Am I saying give away your commissions?

No.

I'm simply trying to get the point across that you don't need to be an affiliate for every product or website you happen to mention to your readers under the guise of trying to help them.

It's really not necessary anyway.

I'm not saying that you shouldn't promote products to your readers. You should. Just don't club them over the head with your offers before they've gotten a chance to get a feel for you and if you're someone who's looking out for their interests or just your own.

Some of the publishers I pay attention to are the ones who from time to time will pass on resources to me just because they think those resources would be of interest to me and my goals. When someone does something for you just because, without appearing to gain anything financially from it, especially online, you take notice.

Perception is about appearances. You have to present yourself as you would like others to see you. If you want others to see you as someone who is giving and truly interested in <u>them</u> and what <u>they</u> want to accomplish then you have to do things that make you look that way.

When you pass on helpful information to your readers because you feel like that information will help them without necessarily promoting a product it accomplishes two things.

|+| Passing on resources to your subscribers without always worrying about your commissions builds trust because they start to think that you want to help them and not just get money from them. **This makes them more willing to give you money when you ask for it**. That's just the way it works.

|+| Prompting your subscribers to send you feedback on the resource(s) you tell them about is what helps to make your list responsive to your future offers. Get your readers used to interacting with you. Get them used to doing what you ask. In order to do that, you have to keep asking them to do stuff.

When you find anything you think is useful and think your subscribers will find useful as well, pass it on to them even if you don't get a commission from a product they buy.

You don't have to do that every single time you write something but do it and ask them for their opinions on what you wrote. Writing to your readers without caring about getting commissions for every single product you mention is a small price to pay in the long run for the level of trust you inspire.

That trust (built on the fact that you have shown your readers they are more than just a dollar sign) is what will set you apart from 99.9% of the other publishers out there.

Let's be real. I publish to profit, but not at the cost of my values and ethical code. I do not subscribe to mentalities that glorify philosophies such as:

"the end justifies the means"

or....

"Get rich or die tryin'"

If my subscribers never buy from me, then I will have to adjust my publishing because business is all about strategy and efficiency as well. I am in business to make money, and it is no secret and if you are reading this book, then you are also in the same mind frame. **It's all in your attitude and your approach.**

What does this mean to your bottom line?

|+| The more you give to your readers without asking for a lot in return the more they'll feel like the NEED to give back to you. That's the law of reciprocation at work. Most of us were taught to give back what we get from people. That being the case, be careful about what you give because what you give is what you can expect to get back. That's a scary thought huh? ;-)

|+| Like I said just a minute ago your subscribers understand that you are in business to make money. If you don't make money, you go out of business. The issue a lot of the time with publishers is that if you haven't

been giving your readers information they actually value, they won't care if you stay in business or not which means they won't bother buying the products you recommend.

I buy products from publishers who do their best to give me value because I want them to stick around. The only way I know how to keep them around is to buy from them.

Give your readers some credit. **They know that to keep you in business they have to buy what you recommend**. The only real question is do you give them enough value in the form of quality information for them to care if you stay in business or not?

The bottom line is you are a person and your subscribers are people. The Internet for all its wonders lacks what many people crave the most, which is to connection with another human being. The Internet is faceless and impersonal. Use that to your advantage.

Be a Real Person to Your Readers

Whenever you create an information product (an article or even just a simple report) do so with the intention of putting together something that will actually help people do something specific. Help people achieve a goal.

Don't worry so much about your commission checks. Those will be there if your readers feel like you've earned them.

You earn them by not making them your focus. Focus on giving value to the people who keep you in business. You can't afford to be one of the many publishers who forget that.

How To Think And Become A Successful Webpreneur

People want to interact with other people online. Especially those who share valuable information. Give your readers those two things (interaction and valuable information) and you'll quickly discover as I have that you magically have more **active readers** instead of just subscribers.

Something that may help ...

Do what I do.

Write as much as you can without using any affiliate links at all.

If you are going to include affiliate links, raise the ethical bar, and tell them that the link you have there is an affiliate link. It is another way of doing business, and it may not give you a windfall of cash in the beginning, but in the long run, your income will explode exponentially!

Focus on providing quality content without distracting yourself with how you will get paid from what you write. After you have the content nailed down you can always go back and add an affiliate link to a good product (you have used) that supports what you've written.

When you become known as someone who gives value, you will be **perceived** as someone who also promotes valuable products. If people feel that the information you give away is bad then they assume that anything you promote is bad as well.

It's all about perception.

Remember that.

Project the image of yourself that you want your readers to see. Want them to see you as someone who cares about them? Then do the things you would do if you did care about them like give them information you KNOW will help them even if you don't get a check from it.

You should care about your readers. Period. Any other approach is not only futile, but it is short term.

Choose your actions wisely. Our actions dictate who we are and who people see us to be.

Like I mentioned earlier when I was talking about habits, if you do something long enough it will become a habit that will now be a part of who you are. Even if at first you have to try to make it **seem** like you care about your readers more than you actually do, eventually you'll notice that you're not faking anymore.

It can be hard to really care about someone who doesn't do things for you (like buy your products) but by focusing on your subscribers' wants and needs they **will** start to put money in your pockets and I guarantee **you'll start to love them** then.

And remember … always do what you do for a specific reason.

You're not giving to your subscribers just for the heck of it. This is your purposeful attempt to show them that you value them and see them as **more** than just a dollar sign.

Doing that allows you (over time) to convert more subscribers into customers because they will WANT to buy from/through you to make sure that you stay in business. If you don't provide your readers with valuable content, they won't care if you stay in business or not so you can kiss your commission checks and main income goodbye.

Give, give, give and then give some more. That's the secret!

Your readers should be so wrapped up in the idea that <u>you</u> **are one of the** *few* **people online who genuinely cares about them and their business** that they will jump at <u>anything</u> you say is worth their time and their money because they have learned that you only tell them about things that you believe will benefit them.

When you can get your readers to believe that (through your past actions) you have their best interests in mind whenever you tell them about a product or point them to a resource, they will learn to **listen to** and **trust** what you say.

But Doesn't Giving Your Readers Free Information Only Train Them To Expect More Free Information From You And Not Buy?

Not really. For two reasons...

1. Your readers know that if they want you to keep producing quality free information for them that they have to buy your products or the products you recommend. It doesn't hurt when you remind them on occasion that your time is valuable and that you'll keep publishing only if it's in your best interest to do so. Kind of like what I did throughout this report.

Like I said earlier, I publish for profit. As soon as it's no longer profitable for me to produce information like this, I'll be forced to stop. If I want to help people, I need to first be in a position to help.

2. People online don't know who you are. You have to demonstrate that you have some knowledge about your supposed area of expertise before they can believe that you know enough to give them recommendations on products that will help them.

If you're just the average publisher who pushes a bunch of recycled articles surrounded by ads, how is that any different from what they do? If you can't offer them any more than they can offer themselves, you become unnecessary.

The main thing people are looking for is guidance from others who **seem** to know something more than they know. The only way people will see

you as that person is for you to show them. If you don't know anything then go out and learn something. Then show others what you've learned. That's all any good teacher does. They are constantly learning something new.

Really what it comes down to is you understanding what people think. People expect you to go after their wallet **without** proving yourself first. People expect your newsletter to be full of "junk" and ads. People expect you to look out for **your** needs first.

Well, guess what??

Surprise them!

Almost Forgot This: When you start asking your subscribers for feedback you need to keep in mind that most of them won't respond, but some will. Maybe a lot of them will. That's a good sign, but it may not seem that way when you start thinking about how you're going to respond to everyone who emails you.

Here's what to do in that situation...

Instead of doing what a lot of people do which is to answer emails for hours at a time, set aside 10-15 minutes and go through all your email 2-4 times a day. It's easier to knock all your email out in blocks than it is to try and handle it in bits and pieces throughout the day.

Set up specific times for getting to your emails and for the most part, stick to that schedule.

The most important part about asking your readers for questions is responding to those questions within a reasonable amount of time. I've had problems with that in the past and it was partly due to me not setting a schedule for checking my email. When you have a schedule, it's easier to have the right mindset to answer the questions you get.

How To Think And Become A Successful Webpreneur

Am I saying that you can't check your email sporadically during the day? No. Sure you can; as long as you mainly stick to whatever schedule you've set for yourself. Any extra time you spend going through your email is entirely up to you.

Important: You might think some of the questions you get from your readers are of little value and you may even think some of them are a waste of your time to answer. However, you should always try to keep in mind the fact that any question someone asks is important to him or her so those questions must become important to **you**.

Think about it. Even though email is easy to send, it still requires some effort to compose an email and send it out. When **you** send email to someone, you expect a timely response because your question or concern is important to you.

Right?

Your readers are no different.

Here's the bottom line...

How do you feel about people who do things for you? Aren't you more willing to do things for people who have already done things to benefit you? Of course you are and if you honestly ask yourself why you'll come to the conclusion that it's because you want those people or that person to continue to **want** to do things for you in the future.

That's how newsletter publishing works.

It's a measured give and take.

When you give you to subscribers they will give to you if only to keep you in the mood to keep giving to them. If all you do is try to take from your subscribers you'll start breed resentment at your attempt to snatch their hard earned money at every chance you get.

Your subscribers buying from you is a direct result of your efforts to make them want to keep you in business so you can continue to do things that benefit them. That's basically it. People care about their needs above and beyond yours so take care of theirs first.

Relationship Marketing Principle #3: Be Yourself Even If Some People Don't Like It

This last rule requires you to be bold. It requires you to expect and accept the fact that some people are going to flat out reject you. If you can't deal with rejection, <u>learn</u> to deal with it.

Trust is a result of people seeing you as a real person willing to share of yourself and not just a automated cloned robot pushing out recycled articles and ads just like everyone else seems to do.

Part of that has to do with the way you write to your readers. You have to write in a way that it looks personal. Like an actual person sat down and took the time to communicate with them. Every single one of your readers knows you have many hundreds or thousands of subscribers but that doesn't mean that you can't **write like only one person is reading**. In fact, that's what you have to do.

One of the easiest ways I've found to learn how to do this is to look at your database of subscribers and pick one to write your letter to. Just one. Then compose your emails in your email client that's addressed to just that one subscriber.

It's a little intimidating, but you can also just imagine that you're writing to one of your bigger competitors which forces you to put some real effort into the information you present. It kind of forces you to raise your game a bit.

How To Think And Become A Successful Webpreneur

No matter how many people you write to, only one person is reading your email at a time so it's important that it **"sounds" like** you're writing to that one person.

Personal stories help as well because they help solidify that fact that you are a real person. There's too much use of the word "we" online. If you're the only person running your business then who is "we"? Carefully remove the stick and relax.

If it's just you, say I or me when you write.

There's nothing wrong with that because again, anything that allows people to picture you having a one on one conversation with them goes a long way towards helping you build a relationship with them.

Now here's the thing...

I have to clear this up because I know it's something that may confuse you. When I say write personal **stories I don't mean you have to talk about personal things**. It's not necessary to do that. What I mean is talk about something that isn't about your online business or if it is about your business, do it with your own words and personality.

The more personal you can get your newsletter to look, the more your readers will start to respond to you. You see, you've been told to build your list and send out a newsletter and of course you should, but why should you? Do you know why? Has anyone ever told you why?

The #1 goal is to build a relationship with like-minded people who seek guidance on the way to their goals. Your job is to help them get to wherever they want to go. All people care about is where they want to go and if you can help them get there.

Your job is not to send out a bunch of recycled articles and ads. People don't want that and the thing is, many of them won't unsubscribe when you send them junk. They will just stop listening to you.

So, even though you may appear to have thousands of subscribers, **you actually don't** because many of them have quit reading. You have to ask yourself, why should anyone care about you or what you have to say or even relate to you and your business?

Do you give them a reason to? If you don't, start.

People don't care about or relate to robots.

They care about and relate to other **real** people.

Here are the two things you need to absolutely include in your newsletters in terms of approach and mindset :

1. Make the first part of it personal. Talking about yourself is OK, but more importantly it is talking about what your reader needs in your own words. This allows your reader to really interact with what you are saying and get a feel for who you really are.

2. Write your own articles. This is where it is important to care for your readers and customers. When you write your own articles, your genuine care and concern will transpire pas the details and facts that you will give. Make people feel like they know you and you will stand head and shoulders above the crowd.

Standing out online is a good thing. You need to rise above the crowd and show people **why** they should be dealing with **you** over someone else. If you don't, your competitors will be on equal ground with you and you don't want that. You want a person to see you as having no competition because they **feel** **like** they know you and that you are someone who wants to help them achieve **their** goals.

"Personality" is one of the most under used tools in the Internet business arena. Of course, Right alongside personality is good content.

You need to balance the one with the other. You won't be able to produce a loyal customer following without good quality content.

If you don't feel you can write good content for your newsletter, then use other people's articles ethically (credit them). Just keep in mind your primary goal is :

"To build relationships with prospects and turn them into customers."

You can use other people's articles when you write but surround those articles with enough of your own information to get people to **feel like** they are connecting with **you** on some level. Most publishers don't take the time to do this, which is why **you** have to.

Don't be a Sleazy SALES SCHMUCK!!

A lot of the email I get is from people who are trying **way too hard** to sell me something. In other words, they really want my money and it shows. I can almost smell the desperation in their email and being desperate to get something from people is a surefire way to make them not want to give it to you at all!

When you desperately want something another person can give you (no matter what it is) you attach an extreme amount of value to that thing and it makes them not want to let it go because whatever you're asking for **now** has more value than they thought.

People hold onto things of value.

I'll give you an example.

Have you ever offered someone something you personally didn't see much value in and they got a little too excited about it? Didn't it make you reconsider giving it away?

That's because that thing you were just about to casually give away apparently has more value than you thought.

As soon as people sense they have something you desperately want, they either won't give it to you or they'll make you work too hard to get it. Just from my own personal observations I've found that people like to hold onto things that **other** **people find valuable** even if those things have no real value to **them**.

You have to detach yourself from the outcome of what you're doing.

When you write to people, write **because you** **want to** and because **you** **want to help** **them**. In other words, you should try to never tip your hand and show how much you really want something they have if you expect any fair chance of getting it.

Of course you want to present your product offers but when you present an offer without putting all kinds of crazy expectations in your head about how much money you're going to make, you won't come off like you desperately need people to buy from you.

People always want to feel like they're doing something for **their** reasons and **not** because you "forced" them into a decision.

Your main focus should be on writing something helpful even when you're making a product offer. Give people some information they can use even if they don't buy from you.

Think about that the next time you write. When you write with the idea in your head that it doesn't really matter if people order or not because you're writing to help them, the action you want them to take won't have a feeling of desperation (or added value) attached to it.

I guarantee that when you create a newsletter, special report, or anything else for that matter with the mindset of helping people and not on selling a million copies that people will in turn not only buy from you but praise your efforts and tell other people about your work.

How To Think And Become A Successful Webpreneur

Remember: People care about themselves first, then anyone else who seems to care about them too. So when you do things for the people who are giving you their time, (reading what you write) they learn to value what you say and do things to benefit you so that you feel like continuing to do things for them. It's not about **you** at all.

What usually gets you in trouble is the fact that you're thinking about yourself and what **you're** trying to accomplish. That keeps you from seeing the fact that if you want other people to give you what you want, you have to give them what they want first.

The One Question You Need to Ask Yourself

I've given you a lot of insight into my thought process when I approach a writing project but none of what I shared with you will help you at all if you can't honestly answer this question...

Are you willing to put what you want to the side and focus on giving others what they want without thinking so much about how much you're going to get paid from your efforts?

That's a tricky question because even if you answer yes, that's not enough. Saying what you're willing to do and being willing to do what you say are two <u>completely</u> different things.

Your major competitors are seen as people who have products that are superior to just about anything you produce. Why? Because nearly all of them understand everything I've told you up to this point.

Respect the time other people are willing to share with you by giving them the best information you possibly can. Forget about competition and that if you give away or sell some of your best information that it's going to hurt you and your business.

That's crazy because most of the people you share your information with won't do a damn thing with it. Out of every 100 people you could probably expect 5 people **or less** to go through all of it and put together a plan they will actually execute.

But here's the thing.

For every 100 people who buy your products only a small percentage of them will do enough to compete with you on any level whatsoever. So about 95 people out of the 100 who gave you their money won't do anything at all to put a dent in your business.

People get addicted to stuff that makes them feel good. When you produce quality information that's geared towards actually helping people, many of them will get a **wishful thinking high**. What I mean by that is they'll sit there with your materials and daydream about your information helping them to do something but they won't actually put any of your information to good use.

Just having a great product in their possession is enough for them.

These types of people like to create ideal outcomes in their heads and scare themselves out of taking action because if they took action, they would be accountable/responsible for their own future.

I'm not sure where it comes from but people love to blame others for their past, current and future states. People don't take responsibility for their actions anymore. At least, they don't want to. **As long as that mindset exists, you can produce highly valuable products and sell them to a lot of people knowing that <u>you</u> <u>are</u> <u>not</u> creating a large number of competitors**.

With that being said, there's no reason for you to hold back the quality of anything you produce. Most people will say a lot of things but they aren't willing to do a lot of the things they say. They talk about taking action on good information but they won't.

So sell thousands of high quality products and count your money. Holding back on the quality of your information ultimately limits the number of repeat customers you'll have and takes money out of **your** pockets so don't hold back. Give people the mental high they want and deposit the money you get into your bank account.

You're not responsible for anyone else's success. If they don't want to do what it takes to be successful, that's completely on **them**, but do give them quality products that work if they work them.

Ignore Them and Keep Moving Forward
Nobody likes rejection or criticism.

It absolutely terrifies most people and that's why many of them will never get anywhere in business or in life. No matter what you do you run the risk of being criticized or rejected by other people.

Every single time you create an article, newsletter, eCourse or report you put yourself in a position for someone to criticize you. That one fact alone stops most people in their tracks before they can even start because everybody (on some level) wants to be accepted.

Not everyone is going to like what you put out there so you need to come to terms with that right now and understand that you're not alone. Even the gurus get a little nervous when they release something to the masses. You just have to be willing to push through that fear.

You'll soon start to realize (as I did) that the majority of people will appreciate your efforts and look to encourage you on to bigger and better things. Forget the losers who have nothing better to do than to tear someone else down so they can feel taller.

Success comes to those who plan for it and are bold enough to go after it no matter who stands in their way. Plan for success then boldly move forward with your plan no matter what.

I'm not the greatest writer in the world but at the same time, I don't ask anyone for permission to write and be successful at it.

Don't ask for permission to succeed and don't worry about how people will react to your work. As long as you take the time to make sure you do your best, you have reason to be proud of yourself.

Everyone had to start somewhere and the people who would criticize you the harshest only want to keep you down so you don't ever develop the skills needed to compete with them. Ignore them and keep moving forward towards your goals.

"Never let anyone take your accomplishments (big or small) away from you. Just keep moving forward."

The Power of First Impressions

You've probably heard the saying… ***"You never get a second chance to make a good first impression"*** and it's very true.

The first contact you have with someone is sometimes your only chance to get them to see you as you want to be seen so it's critically important that you put some thought into that first contact.

What people believe is true <u>is</u> <u>the</u> <u>truth</u> as far as they're concerned. That being the case, your job is to influence (right from the start) what people think the truth is.

Some of the people I've shared this view with say it's unethical to try and make people believe something that isn't necessarily true and I agree because that's not what I'm asking you to do.

How To Think And Become A Successful Webpreneur

I'm asking you to actually have **honest intentions** with people and take measured steps to make them see those intentions where they would normally assume something bad. Never let people assume something about you. Let them know what you want them to know upfront so it's easier for them to let their guard down around you.

Just think about it.

How many promotional emails have you gotten this week about some new product? How many of those publishers routinely send you helpful information without trying to make a sales pitch?

Not many.

Whenever you see who some emails are from you automatically know it's a sales pitch and your guard goes up. You aren't likely to buy from that person when this happens.

That's why I stress the need to **send your readers more than a flood of affiliate links**. That's a big key to getting more people to buy from you right there. If you write a report about doing something specific and get people excited about it, they'll want to buy a product that helps them do what you just got them excited about doing.

Anything you can do to distance yourself from competitors like that can only help you make more money. Your readers expect you to be like everyone else. Don't be.

You have no excuse for continuing to do what you've always done and getting yourself lumped into a pile with the rest of your competitors. You know better. You know what steps to take. All that's left is for you to make a decision right now to take action on them.

The future of marketing on the Internet will be based on building relationships - authentic and sincere relationships.

Adding value, sharing, empowering and giving will be the new currency.

Richard Essi

Hype will soon be a thing of the past, people will demand more and more detailed attention, and will be less tolerant of flukes, and superficial people!

There are people waiting for you to express that which only you can express. So, go out there with your unique story, and make your voice heard.

To Your Ethical Success,

ABOUT RICHARD ESSI

In his short but 36 years on this earth, Richard has had the privilege of living and visiting several countries around the world. A few of these countries include: The United Kingdom, Scotland, Switzerland (where he now lives), The United States of America, Sierra Leone, Germany, Holland, France, Bulgaria, Belgium, Sweden, Burundi, Cameroon, Guadeloupe, Denmark, Equatorial Guinea, Italy, Canada, and many more scheduled.

Richard Essi is above all titles a happily married husband and a proud father of two. Richard is a natural motivator, a passionate and results oriented life coach who firmly believes that the value of each human on this earth is priceless, and that there is no single human being on this earth who is just an "accident".

Richard firmly believes that life is meant to be lived with purpose. While not considering himself religious, Richard is highly RELATIONAL. He chooses authenticity over superficiality. He has tried and proven in his life that giving authentically and unselfishly far outweighs in satisfaction anything he has ever received.

www.ingramcontent.com/pod-product-compliance
Lightning Source LLC
Chambersburg PA
CBHW051317170526
45166CB00002B/578